thinking
for
learning

MEL ROCKETT
SIMON **&** **PERCIVAL**

The authors would like to thank the following for providing help and materials in producing this book:

Allendale First School

Allendale Middle School

Blyth Community College

Byrness First School

Cheshire Local Education Authority (Peter Greenhalgh)

Department for Education and Skills

The Discovery Project

Dukes Middle School

Haydon Bridge High School

Hempnall First School, Hempnall, Norfolk

Hipsburn First School

Kenton High School

Kinsale Avenue First School, Norwich

Larkman First School, Norwich

Norfolk Education Advisory Service (Helen Banks)

Northumberland LEA

Paulsgrove Primary School, Portsmouth

Portsmouth City Education Department

Prudhoe Community High School

Ryles Park High School, Macclesfield

St Benet Biscop RC High School, Bedlington

Stobhillgate First School

Teacher Training Agency (TTA)

Thinking Skills Research Centre, University of Newcastle (Vivienne Baumfield)

Thomas Tallis School, Greenwich

Tuckswood First School, Norwich

Wylam First School

Published by
Network Educational Press Ltd
PO Box 635
Stafford
ST16 1BF
www.networkpress.co.uk

Managing Editor: Janice Baiton
Design: Neil Hawkins – Network Educational Press Ltd
Illustrations: Trevor Bounford – bounford.com
Printed in Great Britain by
MPG Books Ltd., Bodmin, Cornwall.

Contents

Foreword

The *Accelerated Learning Series* attempts to pull together new and innovative thinking about learning. The titles in the series offer contemporary solutions to old problems. The series is held together by the accelerated learning model which, in turn, is underwritten by an informed theoretical understanding.

The term 'Accelerated Learning' can be misleading. The method is not for a specific group of learners, nor for a given age range, nor for a category of perceived ability. The method is not about doing the same things faster. It is not about fast-tracking or about hot-housing. It is a considered, generic approach to learning based on research drawn from disparate disciplines and tested with different age groups and different ability levels in very different circumstances. As such, it can be adapted and applied to very different challenges.

The books in the *Accelerated Learning Series* build from the Accelerated Learning Cycle. The cycle starts by attending to the physical, environmental and social factors in learning. It proposes the worth of a positive and supportive learning environment. It then deliberately attempts to connect to, and build upon, prior knowledge and understanding whilst presenting an overview of the learning challenge to come. Participants set positive outcomes and define targets towards reaching those outcomes. Information is then presented in visual, auditory and kinesthetic modes and is reinforced through different forms of intelligent response. Frequent, structured opportunities to demonstrate understanding and to rehearse for recall are the concluding feature of the cycle.

In March 2001 this question appeared on the Swiss National Census form,

'In which language do you think?'

A good question and not one that we would see on a UK Census form. Does the language of your thought indicate the nature of the thought? The authors tell the story of a bilingual teenager with a French mother and an English father. Asked about her thinking, she pointed out that if she wanted to think coolly and rationally, she thought in English like her father. If she wanted to think emotionally and with feeling, she thought in French like her mother.

Is there a language of thinking? If so, can that language be taught? How should it be taught? By whom? When? Do we know all the languages of thought? Are there more? Why is there such an interest now? Is there such a thing as a thinking skill? What about a thinking classroom? A thinking school?

◆ The emergence of interest in thinking skills

In the UK there has been an unexpected growth in interest in 'thinking skills'. The term 'thinking' is now common parlance in the UK learning community in a way that was unfashionable ten or more years ago. We now have Local Education Authority posts advertised for 'Thinking Co-ordinator KS3'. Perhaps we shall shortly see the emergence of Head of Thinking posts in schools with attached responsibility points. The underground movements around Philosophy for Children, Somerset Thinking Skills and CASE have suddenly emerged, blinking, into the full stare of the country. Why is there such an interest now?

We have a one-size-fits-all education system where teachers struggle heroically to differentiate, to build in continuity and progression, and to assess against a battery of levels. Yet at the same time, we know more and more about the individuality of learning. Recent challenges to orthodox views regarding intelligence have left us believing that, rather than be an inherited lump determined by genetic inheritance, intelligence may well be modifiable, that it may evidence itself in multiple ways and at different developmental stages: perhaps it could even be taught.

We have an emerging fascination with neuroscience. Professors of neurology have become media personalities. The science tells us of the complexity, plasticity and adaptability of the human brain. It now shows us how new cells can in fact be grown. It demonstrates how neural structures are modified throughout the life span by experience.

Educationalists have re-discovered constructivism and, in particular Vygotsky's very early work on scaffolding and proximal development. Constructivists argue that one only understands information relative to what one already understands, meaning being constructed from one's own experiences.

Perhaps most significantly there is an impatience amongst professionals and, dare it be said, even amongst some politicians, with a content curriculum and a recognition that an obsession with 'knowing' will betray us in the future when it's the 'learners' who will prevail. The political tension is self-evident. Societies change. Every considered view based on meaningful evidence points to the fact that learning requires active engagement. Children need to be stretched and challenged. Cramming with content squeezes out the active engagement. However, to engage actively means involving, it means independent decision-making and it means electing through choice. A content curriculum by its very nature is at odds with this. A preoccupation with end testing has the same effect. Summative assessment squeezes out formative, and yet it is formative assessment – learning as you go – that works.

Emerging, and alternative models, of teaching and learning have recently secured the interest of the educators and generated much debate. None more so than the accelerated learning model. It has its critics but even they would acknowledge it has done a job in getting a community discussing the nature of learning and the paucity of some of our inherited models. It has played a part in clearing the ground for work on thinking skills and formative assessment. We now have national projects with popular appeal that focus on learning about learning. At the same time thinking from business and research communities has begun to shape the educator's interest: emotional intelligence, collaborative learning, coaching and mentoring.

◆ What are thinking skills?

Is there a language of thinking? If so, what are the languages and are there skills that go with the languages? Can a process that is cognitive be described as a skill? The term is ambiguous. How do I demonstrate the skill? At what point ought it to emerge? Should such a skill, displaced from its context, be given value? We are told by the old and the sage that, 'there are many ways to skin a cat'. No doubt there are and no doubt I could develop my skills as a cat skinner, but should I be doing this anyway?

The language of thinking has common points. Researchers such as McGuiness and also Schwartz and Parks acknowledge the difficulty in isolating a set of 'skills' but nevertheless offer a range that includes:

* Sequencing and ordering information
* Sorting, classifying, grouping
* Analysing, identifying relationships
* Comparing and contrasting
* Making predictions and hypothesising
* Drawing conclusions
* Distinguishing facts and opinion
* Bias and reliability
* Generating ideas and brainstorming
* Cause and effect, fair tests
* Defining and clarifying problems
* Thinking up solutions
* Goals and sub-goals
* Testing solutions, evaluating outcomes
* Planning and monitoring
* Making decisions
* Setting priorities
* Pros and cons
* Reflecting on one's own thinking.

As with all languages, they are only genuinely useful within a context. Although the above list could be said to supply us with all the essential grammar, it's when we have to use it, retain it and transfer it that it works its magic. Can we take these skills or 'language elements' and organise them into families? This would be akin to mapping a family such as the different European languages. We can organise the thinking skills approaches into three families. They could be:

1 The teaching of specific skills outside of a domain
* Instrumental Enrichment (Feuerstein, Sharron)
* Somerset Thinking Skills (Blagg)
* Top Ten Thinking Tactics (Lake and Needham)

2 The teaching of skills within a subject domain
* CASE/CAME – Cognitive Acceleration in Science/Maths Education (Adey and Shayer)
* Thinking through Geography (Leat)

3 The teaching of thinking skills across domains
* ACTS (Activating Children's Thinking Skills)
* Infusion of Thinking into Subject Content (Schwartz and Parks)

8

* CORT (De Bono)
* Philosophy for Children (Lipman, Fisher, Murris)
* De-briefing (Leat and others)
* Accelerated Learning (Smith, Rose)
* Multiple Intelligence (Gardner)

Is there overlap between the languages? Do the thinking skills approaches have similarities? Of course they do, otherwise we have major problems! They are all, in their own way and with their own philosophical and pedagogical approach, trying to develop some of the language units or skills described in our list above.

◆ Can thinking skills be taught? Is it worth the effort?

It has to be more than an act of faith that thinking can be taught. The current research evidence as to how and when and for what duration is confused and, I would argue, contaminated by poor controls. We await independent research that acts on tight controls and has a set of meaningful outcomes to measure against. Much of the research is conducted by those who are promoting their own programmes. It is insufficient to say that improvements in GCSE scores arising from a thinking skills approach means that there are concomitant and permanent improvements in thinking. The GCSE exams measure a different set of qualities. Some say that, in its current form, it is largely a memory test. How do we measure transferability?

With a heavy investment in teacher development for some of the thinking skills programmes – as much as eight working days over six terms – one would expect a significant return but what we get is often patchy. Gains in self-esteem, behaviour, risk-taking, collaboration, listening and questioning skills, and reflective thinking are all notoriously difficult to measure. This doesn't mean the journey isn't worth it but before you set out know the pros and cons. Here are a few:

The evidence for the teaching of thinking skills

★ some evidence of success with children in profound learning disadvantage (IE)
★ the proponents argue for general transferability of skills
★ acquisition and retention of thinking skills offer a lifelong learning advantage
★ proponents (of IE) argue it is possible and desirable to separate skills of thinking from the content or domain
★ some evaluations show improvement in related academic performance (CASE)
★ some small-scale experiments show improvement in idea generation (CORT)
★ it leads to improvement in the professional knowledge of teachers
★ it is what successful teachers do!
★ successful prototypes exist and are in place.

The evidence against the teaching of thinking skills

✧ the definition of thinking skills remains problematic
✧ the narrowness of definitions of thinking skills do not ally to breadth of interpretation of 'intelligence'
✧ insufficient evidence of transfer across subjects or domains

✧ the more general a skill, the less useful it is

✧ teaching thinking skills does not necessarily develop dispositions towards their use

✧ some evaluations of 'successful' programmes are insufficiently objective

✧ thinking skills can be too readily positioned as a 'bolt-on' activity

✧ successful prototypes have worked in 'favourable' learning environments.

◆ How and when should thinking skills be taught?

This book succeeds because of its honesty in proposing a plural approach. It scans the horizon and concludes that there is no one way that sticks out as being exceptional and which every teacher must follow. The two obvious models are those that support specific programmes and those that support infusion.

School circumstances vary and, in some instances, an off-the-shelf package is what is needed. In other cases it may be possible to infuse problem solving, higher order thinking and more reflection into and across subjects. This is a bit like the nozzle on your shower. Do you narrow the flow of water so it concentrates in a spurt onto a narrow spot on your back? It hurts a bit for a while, but it isn't half invigorating. Or do you open up the flow so it disperses over a wider area? It's less intense, less focused, hits more of your body, but is less fun. Is there a right answer? No, it depends on the outcomes you seek. *Thinking For Learning* helps you make the decision.

Looking at the evidence from *Thinking For Learning* and other sources, certain broad pointers emerge as to how and when to develop formal thinking approaches. Here are some:

✭ Start early – neuroscience talks of sensitive periods for neural development where structures are beginning to be laid in place for life starting and ending early.

✭ Begin broad then narrow – Philosophy for Children encourages teachers to model Socratic dialogue in the context of broad choices and decisions faced by characters in novels.

✭ Root the skills in context – this means that we may develop the skills in our own subject discipline but we always de-brief for transfer and use in different contexts.

✭ Put the spotlight on metacognition – encourage learners to share and evaluate their thinking within, throughout and after the experience: Accelerated Learning proponents call this pole-bridging.

✭ Encourage and plan for co-operation and shared decision-making.

✭ Become a coach, a mentor and a model for the practices you espouse.

✭ Encourage dialogue to develop listening and questioning skills.

✭ Develop process sensitivity – explain why you are doing what you are doing and encourage learners to do the same: share the skills.

✭ Use a range of technologies – including computers – but expose the learning models and methodologies as you do so (many learners 'scratch and sniff' on computers – they do not test themselves on challenging cognitive activities).

I would thoroughly commend *Thinking For Learning* to you. Mel Rockett and Simon Percival have undertaken a large task in describing the language of thinking skills and how the various families relate to each other.

Acknowledgements

MEL ROCKETT

This book is the result of several years' work by groups of teachers in schools in Northumberland and neighbouring LEAs with support from the School of Education, University of Newcastle and the LEA's Standards and Effectiveness Division.

Particular thanks must go to David Leat and Vivienne Baumfield at Newcastle University for the initial inspiration and their on-going enthusiasm and support.

Dozens of teachers have contributed ideas and have trialled and evaluated all sorts of activities. They are far too many to mention but I must single out for special attention the following key influences: Rachel Lofthouse, David Kinninment, Anna Rossiter, Anne DeA'Echevarria, James Nottingham, Tim Stout, Hazel Ward, Ian Patience, Ruth Bradley, Lynn Johnston, Claire Harbottle, Dave Clarke, Simon Chandler, Doug Paterson, Julie McGrane and Marie Butterworth.

The influence of Alistair Smith's work in the field of Accelerated Learning has been pivotal to the continuing development of our work whilst the ideas of Reuven Feuerstein, Howard Gardner and Matthew Lipman have been especially useful.

Many thanks to Deborah Anderson, Anne Carruthers and Pat Oliver for their ability to make sense of my scribbling and their support and good humour. Thanks to Helen Johnston for her creativity and good humour.

Thanks to our editor, Janice Baiton, for her unstinting attention to detail, her sensitive pressure and her creative ideas. And to Jim Houghton of Network Educational Press, a long-standing friend without whom this book would not have been conceived.

And finally special thanks to Cath for her guidance, wisdom and patience.

SIMON PERCIVAL

Additionally I too would like to thank all the teachers who have contributed in some way to this book: those who have allowed me into their schools and classrooms, those who have provided materials, those former colleagues who always inspired and those sages from my youth. Family, friends, and colleagues at Alite, you know who you are, thank you.

Finally, I would like to thank Wendy for her unstinting support and encouragement in all that I do. This is for you.

Thinking

Preview

The need for a relevant and useful education, which prioritises the *how* rather than the *what*

Messages from Curriculum 2000

The second component, Accelerated Learning, and some of its tenets

How schools might accommodate this

Principles underlying the Thinking for Learning approach

This chapter will provide you with explanations of the background to **Thinking**, specifically:

What thinking is

Some of the key Thinking Skills approaches

What skills learners are likely to need in the twenty-first century

Thinking Skills in the National Curriculum

The 'categories' of Thinking Skills

The constituent parts of Thinking for Learning: Thinking Skills and Accelerated Learning

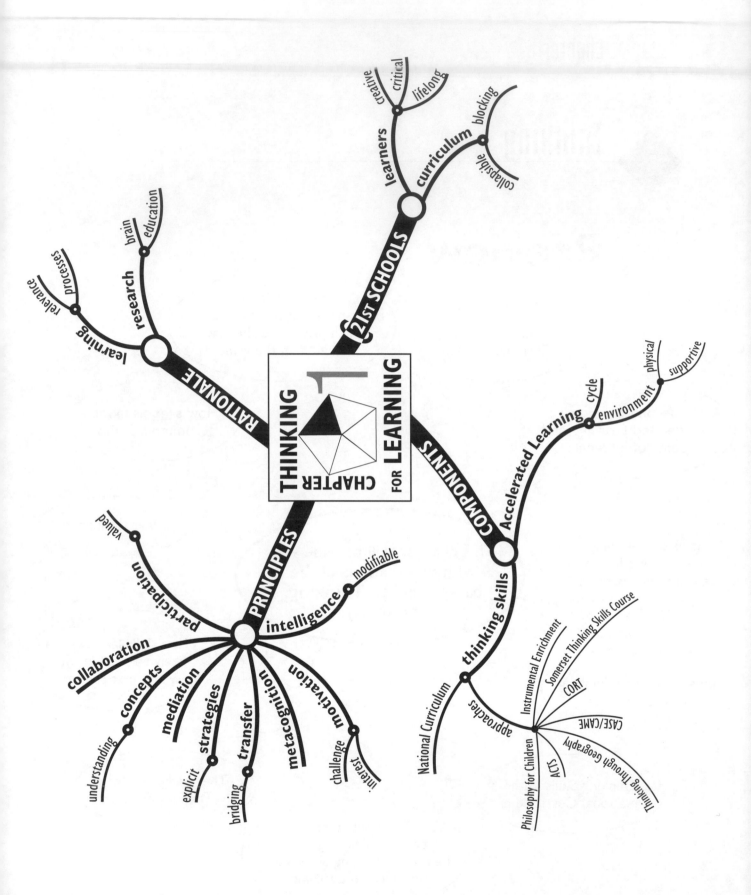

CHAPTER 1

THINKING FOR LEARNING

RATIONALE

[21st SCHOOLS]

learners
- creative
- critical
- lifelong

curriculum
- blocking
- collapsible

learning
- research
  - brain
  - education
- processes
  - relevance

PRINCIPLES

participation
- valued

collaboration

concepts
- understanding

mediation
- explicit

strategies

transfer
- bridging

metacognition

motivation
- challenge
- interest

intelligence
- modifiable

COMPONENTS

Accelerated Learning
- environment
  - cycle
  - physical
  - supportive

thinking skills
- National Curriculum
- approaches
  - Philosophy for Children
  - ACTS
  - Thinking Through Geography
  - CASE/CAME
  - CORT
  - Somerset Thinking Skills Course
  - Instrumental Enrichment

14

Thinking for Learning

◆ Introduction

We all know that a useful education is one that prepares a pupil for the world beyond the school gates. When we were hunter-gatherers, education meant knowing how to trap the evening meal and which berries would not poison us. Now individuals depend upon what competences they can offer potential employers, and employers demand a more flexible and adaptable workforce with the ability to absorb and process information, to draw reasonable conclusions, to make decisions and to create new knowledge.

We are moving into an age when the holding or possession of information is no longer a problem as computers continue to become more powerful and complex. With the processes of production and manufacturing becoming more achievable for all societies, continued wealth will depend upon the ability to generate new ideas and new knowledge, such as in the areas of biotechnology and genetic research. Schools need to nurture the relevant skills in their pupils that will equip them for this challenge, and these should be provided in equal measure to the basic skills.

It is not what pupils learn, but how they learn it that matters. How they learn depends on their cognitive processing capability, and intervention in the process by which this capability develops is the route to fundamental improved life chances in the population of learners.

Adey and Shayer [1]

Just as society needs to generate new ideas about science and production, so schools need to generate new knowledge about learning and organisation. In this new age we need to learn how to innovate.

If the imperative is to know *how* to do things, rather than *what* already exists, then schooling needs to emphasise reflection, ideas and creativity. Pupils will leave schools with many years of learning ahead of them – probably throughout their lives – so they need the skills and dispositions to be able to do this.

Such attributes would not just be of benefit to the individual in the workplace either. Creativity, criticism and reasonableness would be worth encouraging in every citizen for all kinds of reasons.

So can we help foster these competencies in our pupils in order to provide them with a more useful education? Is it possible even with a curriculum laid down by others? The answer to both questions is an emphatic 'Yes!' As we write, there are teachers throughout the country (and elsewhere too) who are using what academic and classroom-based research have shown to be some of the best practice for achieving these aims. In this book we hope to explain these to you, to clarify the ideas that underpin them and to set out a cohesive system that we have come to consider as *Thinking for Learning*.

◆ Schools in the twenty-first century

In many respects most of our schools, and certainly our education system in England and Wales, are still based upon a nineteenth-century model that presumes pupils have quantifiable and static levels of intelligence. It also values traditional 'subjects' more than it does learning, thinking and creativity. Whilst there have been attempts to change this in individual schools and wider learning communities, the basic model persists. We believe that this model will meet the needs of neither the learner nor society in the new millennium.

'The mind is not a vessel to be filled, but a fire to be lighted.'

Plutarch

It is not the purpose of this book to create a model for a new education system, but we believe that a far greater emphasis on creative thinking and on the processes of learning is essential.

Consider the following points:

⌘ Learning begins at birth and continues throughout life as the brain responds to experience and stimulus.

⌘ The brain continues to develop new neural pathways, new knowledge and skills throughout our lives and, particularly, when exposed to new learning experiences.

⌘ The basic skills and the skills and dispositions required for independent and autonomous learning can be learned quite early, during childhood.

⌘ In adolescence young people have the ability and desire to learn independently and to make their own choices.

⌘ The average 5 to 18-year-old spends only about 20 per cent of each school day at school – and only between 5 and 10 per cent of their total time there.

⌘ There is a growing consensus that intelligence is not fixed but is modifiable and that most of us have immense untapped potential for learning.

⌘ All workers will need to learn new skills, as few people today can expect to stay in the same job for their whole working life – and even for those who might, their present skills will become redundant and will need renewing.

The potential is there for shaping creative and critical thinkers in our schools. The modern world of work, and modern life, demands that people should be able to learn. How better to meet that challenge than to show pupils how they learn and to motivate them so that they are open to and excited by the whole experience? Even now, traditional subject lessons can be taught in an innovative, stimulating and relevant manner through Thinking for Learning to encourage this outcome, but what a difference a change of attitudes towards how education is structured would make.

The current National Curriculum (Curriculum 2000) offers a potentially significant move away from an over-emphasis on knowledge retention towards a more balanced view that knowing 'how' is more important than knowing 'what'. This new emphasis on the learning process can be seen in the introductory pages of the primary and secondary handbooks and in the subject orders. So as a preamble to the statutory context there is an emphasis on the importance of 'Key Skills' and 'Thinking Skills'. However, the main initiatives have been:

* National Literacy and Numeracy Strategies

* Citizenship

* Performance Management for Teachers.

These are mainly about the imposition of previously developed and highly structured programmes. However, the twenty-first century is likely to demand the following of learners:

Mastery of Basic Skills (Literacy and Numeracy)

Ability to work with others

Ability to deal with constant distractions and change

Willingness to work in a variety of disciplines and at different levels

Well developed verbal skills

Decision-Making and Problem Solving Skills

John Abbott and Terry Ryan [2]

Certainly the first of these is being addressed through the National Literacy and Numeracy Strategies, which seem to be having a largely positive effect in our primary schools. It remains to be seen whether the same will be true at secondary level. But what about the others?

There are possibilities here and we need to service them. The general requirements of the National Curriculum and the guidance on learning across the curriculum contained within the subject booklets provide an alternative to the detailed programmes of study. We need to shift the emphasis of our teaching away from this content and towards the processes of thinking as outlined under Key Skills, Citizenship, Spiritual, Moral, Social and Cultural Development and other aspects, such as Thinking Skills, work-related learning and education for sustainable development. However, there may be some obstacles:

 Teachers have lived with more than ten years of an over-demanding subject content. Many have been inducted into this system and there is a feeling that OFSTED and others are obsessed with content coverage. The latter may not be true, but it is still a real perception.

2 Because of the over-attention to content coverage and the programmes of study, most teachers are inclined to turn straight to these sections of the National Curriculum Orders, or to the content of the study units provided in the QCA's Schemes of Work. The rhetoric about Thinking Skills gets overlooked.

3 Whilst the statements supporting Thinking Skills are welcome, they do not provide much guidance about what these are or how to promote them. In some cases there is an implication that if the content is hard enough it will promote thinking. Take this example:

RE is an academic subject ... The study of religion is a rigorous activity involving a variety of intellectual disciplines and skills. Skills of research, selection, analysis, interpretation, reflection, empathy, evaluation, synthesis, application, expression and communication are promoted.

QCA [3]

There seems to be little understanding in the National Curriculum documents or the QCA Schemes of Work that there might be a difference between *Thinking* and *Thinking Skills*. Whilst all subjects at school, in fact our whole lives, demand us to think, it is the quality of this thinking and the skills we have to organise our thinking that will make a difference to our achievement and sense of fulfilment.

So, if the new National Curriculum had entirely freed itself from the ancient shackles imposed by earlier attitudes towards education, then the future curriculum models may have looked somewhat different. For example, it is obvious which one of the lists shown opposite would have encouraged the skills, abilities and attitudes outlined in Abbott and Ryan on page 17.

Some schools are beginning to move more towards List B with the 'blocking' of similar subjects together to provide longer periods of contact with pupils, collapsed timetables for a day, a week or longer, challenge and activity weeks, and work-related learning. In Northumberland this can be seen vividly in the work of Cramlington High School,[4] which OFSTED recently described as 'a strikingly successful school'. At Cramlington the principles of Thinking for Learning can be clearly seen in action with significant benefits for pupils.

Both teachers and learners need to develop new sets of skills and attitudes to deal with this changing context. We will explore some of these and their background later in the chapter. But first we need to clarify just what thinking is.

TRADITIONAL: A	OR: B
English	Literacy
Maths	Numeracy
Science	ICT
Geography	Thinking Skills
Modern Foreign Language	Spiritual, Moral, Social
History	and Cultural Development
Technology	Citizenship
ICT	Problem-solving
Music	Sustainable Development
Art	
Physical Education	
Religious Education	

List B developed within distinct subjects	Subjects (A) provide context
Timetables constructed as pieces to be fitted together	Timetable flexible and holistic

◆ What is thinking?

A bilingual girl – English father, French mother – in a Surrey school was recently asked what language she thought in. She considered this for a moment, then replied, 'Well, it depends. If I'm doing something practical, I think in English, but if it involves feelings, then I automatically think in French.'

Such is the nature of thinking. Increasingly, we are able to identify areas of the brain and explain their functions, but what *thinking* is can be more complex to identify. In the example above, the girl was able to classify roughly the situations in which she would think in each language. But what does that mean? Is thinking a stream of words? The novelists Virginia Woolf and James Joyce wanted to show to their readers, as faithfully as possible, what was going through the heads of characters. Could they have been entirely satisfied with the results? And is thinking always such a conscious action? Clearly it is not. How else could you explain those 'A-ha!' moments, as the name of the actress you saw on TV last night pops into your head even though you had consciously given up trying to remember it before you went to bed?

The more you think about it, the more questions are raised. How about when you remember where you last saw your keys? Your thoughts do not provide an elaborate description of the keys bunched on top of the dressing table amongst the brushes, aftershave, perfumes and make-up. Most people would see an image in their 'mind's eye'. And intuition. Is that thinking?

Most psychologists agree that thinking can be divided into two categories: 'propositional' thought and 'imaginal' thought.[5] The former refers to when we 'hear' the words in our mind, the latter to when we 'see' images. Both of these modes are valid in Thinking for Learning. For example, propositional thought can be used in reasoning activities, as it organises our thoughts; imaginal thought can be used for visualisation and creative tasks.

However, children thinking does not in itself equate to meaningful thinking taking place and so Thinking for Learning cannot be considered to be occurring any time that thinking happens in the classroom. First, we have already noted that we all think all the time. Second, this is not as straightforward as encouraging pupils to think in particular ways. The concepts that underpin this approach come together in a set of key principles that should be adhered to if it can truly be said that Thinking for Learning is taking place.

◆ Painting the 'Thinking for Learning' picture

The term 'Thinking for Learning' was coined to describe a blend of particular approaches used to produce more effective learning. Its two main constituent parts are Thinking Skills and Accelerated Learning.[7] Each highlights the importance of process in education, encouraging pupils to understand their learning and so making the strategies of each eminently transferable.

Thinking skills

Thinking Skills support active cognitive processing which makes for better learning. Thus pupils are equipped to search out meaning and impose structure, to deal systematically, yet flexibly, with novel problems and situations; to adopt a critical attitude to information and argument; and to communicate effectively.

McGuinness [8]

For 'active' we could substitute 'conscious'. All thinking is active – the brain making its millions of unique connections in every individual – but Thinking Skills teachers attempt to make students more conscious of their thinking and the strategies they can employ to help them make better meanings.

'Thinking Skills' is a generic term used to describe the collection of such strategies. Although the emphasis is on process, like all the Thinking for Learning strands, subject knowledge is not treated with disdain. If anything it can be argued that knowledge 'is the result of a process of interpretation requiring action and reflection and is achieved in particular social and cultural contexts'.[9] Like all outcomes of reasoning it should be viewed critically, but treated with respect.

Some teachers have an almost instinctive feeling for Thinking Skills strategies. They believe in this style of learning and have a desire to see it work. Others are more sceptical, or open-minded. They need more tangible evidence before they will embark on such strategies. It is in the nature of the real world of education that absolute proofs are very difficult to come by. However, as Carol McGuinness reports in *From Thinking Skills to Thinking Classrooms*[8] there is now a considerable volume of evidence that suggests that various Thinking Skills programmes have a significant impact on pupil achievement. What is not yet certain is whether such strategies can have the same impact if applied across a wider spectrum of teachers and pupils.

We will not be attempting to draw a comprehensive picture of the whole Thinking Skills movement, but instead we will examine some of the key approaches that have informed our interest, how these might be categorised, applied and which Thinking Skills the National Curriculum feels are important.

Instrumental Enrichment (IE)

A seminal influence on those involved in Thinking Skills has been the work of Dr Reuven Feuerstein in Israel. Initially, working with traumatised Jewish adolescents from Europe, North Africa and Asia, Feuerstein recognised that conventional schooling was unable to unlock or develop the potential of many students who were branded as uneducable. He surmised that these students, because of their history, had missed out on a key aspect of learning – that of effective *mediation*.

Without a teacher or other facilitator to help interpret or mediate the experiences of the learner, response to stimulus is unstructured and often incomprehensible.

When this mediation has been lacking for a significant time, only intensive remediation will bring the learner back on track to meeting their real potential.

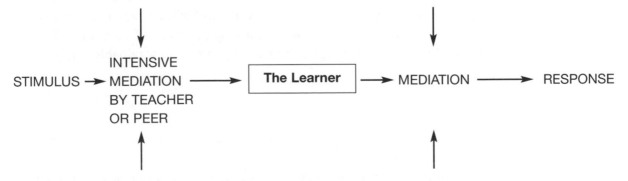

This **mediation** helps to shape and filter our experience in order to make sense of it.

Feuerstein developed teaching aids that he called 'Instruments of Enrichment'. These included Analytical Perception, Categorisation, Instructions and others that were utilised in particular ways. When used intensively by himself and other teachers in controlled environments, these helped many of his students to make remarkable progress:[10]

❑ Ninety impaired students in Israel caught up by *three years* on average when taught IE for one year.[50]

❑ Teaching physics to first-year medical students in New York – 50 per cent failure rate reduced to 0 per cent![49]

Somerset Thinking Skills Course (STSC)

Though there are teachers in the UK who are trained in Instrumental Enrichment (IE), by the mid-1980s it had failed to make a major impact. Research into why this was the case was carried out in Somerset during the mid-to-late 1980s and led to the development and publication of the Somerset Thinking Skills Course.[11] This development took some of the principles of IE and tried to develop them in a context that was felt to be more suitable for the English state school system. Three types of instruments were used in this course – Stimulus Material, Abstract Exercises and Real-life Scenarios – and lessons had a distinctive pattern.

Whilst many schools have adopted the Somerset Course for pupils in Year 7 to Year 9, it has not enjoyed huge success overall. Some feel that this is caused by the very structure of the curriculum in England, which puts so much stress on the separate subject disciplines and the content of these subjects at the expense of a sufficient focus on learning skills.

Cognitive Research Trust (CORT) thinking

In traditional schooling there is one gateway to success – LITERACY. Most pupils pass through this gateway by the age of seven. For those who fail to pass through the future promises low self-esteem, poor motivation and a cycle of failure. **Thinking Skills** offer an alternative gateway. Pupils can succeed with resulting gains in self-esteem and motivation. The literacy gateway then becomes an attainable target.

De Bono (CORT publicity materials)

As both IE and STSC were developing, so was the work of the Cognitive Research Trust in Dublin under the leadership of Edward de Bono. He has published many books on the subject and proposes a range of techniques for developing better thinking for learners of all ages. Again, the impact in schools in the UK has been minimal, although seven million students worldwide have used the course.

Working in Queensland, Australia, John Edwards noted very significant gains amongst a group of 12-year-olds who were taught all the CORT lessons during their last year in primary school (the equivalent of Year 7 in the UK). The table below shows their achievement at the end of the year.

Test	Proportion of pupils scoring above the mean			
	National (%)	School (%)	CORT Group (%)	Difference (%)
Learning ability	31.0	39.5	52.0	+12.5
Study skills	31.0	31.2	48.0	+16.8
Maths skills	31.0	24.8	52.0	+27.2
Language vocabulary	31.0	42.8	62.4	+19.6
Language comprehension	31.0	35.8	50.0	+14.2

Five years later the same students significantly outscored their 'control' peers at the end of secondary school.[51]

Cognitive Acceleration in Science Education (CASE)

During the late 1980s, staff at Kings College, London, developed a programme of Thinking Skills interventions that were located within one of the major subject domains – science.

At the time, science was a high profile subject in the education debate and there was widespread concern about the levels of knowledge and understanding in the subject and the levels of qualifications amongst school leavers.

Under the leadership of Michael Shayer and Philip Adey,[1] the Cognitive Acceleration in Science Education (CASE) project was introduced into a significant number of schools throughout the country. The evidence they have amassed through some complex calculations seems to show very significant gains in attainment for most, but not all, pupils who experienced these materials in Key Stage 3.

Several thousand students in a national project were taught CASE lessons for two years (one lesson per fortnight) during Years 7 and 8, or 8 and 9. At GCSE these pupils achieved up to one grade higher than the control group. These pupils also did significantly better in their English GCSE and in most other subjects.[12]

Subject	Boys 1989		Girls 1990	
	CASE	Control	CASE	Control
Science	41.7	12.8	50.0	33.3
Mathematics	49.1	16.4	55.16	42.42
English	44.6	16.1	85.18	58.06

Percentage GCSE grades C and above

The CASE project produces its own teaching materials and an intensive training course is provided for CASE teachers. Coaching in the techniques is a major component of this training. As the research of Joyce and Showers[13] indicated in the 1980s, classroom support and coaching seems to be essential for the effective professional development of teachers.

Following the perceived success of CASE (Thinking Science), an equivalent course has been developed for Mathematics (CAME – Thinking Maths), and developments are taking place in Technology (CATE).

Thinking Through Geography

At the University of Newcastle the PGCE geography tutor, David Leat, was becoming interested in the work of CASE and wondered how it might be applied in geography teaching. Without the resources to develop an equivalent of CASE – and seeing the scope for a more infused approach to developing pupils' thinking – Dr Leat began to devise and trial materials with his PGCE students and their work in schools.[14] These materials were designed around 'foundation concepts' key to geography.

By 1995 a number of newly qualified geography teachers were making their presence felt in schools throughout the North East. In Northumberland a group of interested humanities teachers formed a network, which has continued to develop and grow since then. Most of the teachers involved report significant benefits from the introduction of Thinking Skills strategies. These include higher attainment in GCSE examinations, increased pupil motivation and enhanced teaching skills.

Nick Chapman, teaching geography at Kenton High School in Newcastle upon Tyne, researched the GCSE examination results of pupils in 12 schools in the North East of England where at least one teacher was using Thinking Skills strategies as part of their repertoire. In comparison with colleagues who rarely or never used such strategies, the Thinking Skills teachers produced GCSE results between 0.4 and 0.6 of a grade better.

Thinking Skills strategies have been effectively introduced from Reception classes through to Sixth Form. This work has led to two publications[15, 16] and the inclusion of Thinking for Learning as a key priority in Northumberland's Education Development Plan for promoting effective teaching and learning.

Activating Children's Thinking Skills [ACTS]

Developed in Northern Ireland for upper primary level use,[17] ACTS teachers use their training to identify areas of the curriculum for which Thinking Skills strategies can be designed and implemented. There is a particular emphasis on thinking diagrams to help make thinking explicit, with questioning and reflecting used to help develop the language needed to discuss and describe the thinking process. These lessons are scripted and are influenced by the work of Swartz and Parks.[18]

Philosophy for Children [P4C]

Originating from the work of Matthew Lipman[6] in the USA, Philosophy for Children advocates a methodology for encouraging pupils to think about ethical and moral issues that interest them with the aim of developing 'reasonableness'. P4C is not a study of the work of philosophers, but an attempt to engage pupils in enquiry and discussion. In a supportive environment, pupils are encouraged to ask and respond to questions, thinking critically about opinions that they and others hold. Many schools use P4C for affective development, which can result in raising individuals' self-esteem and decreasing occurrences of bullying.

Over the years, P4C has been developed by practitioners in more than 30 countries. It is promoted in the UK by SAPERE (the Society for the Advancement of Philosophical and Ethical Reflection in Education).[19]

Details of some of these approaches in practice can be found in Chapter 4.

Categorisation of thinking skills

Approaches to teaching Thinking Skills can be categorised into four types of course:

1 'Bolt-on' generic courses such as Somerset Thinking Skills and the Top Ten Thinking Tactics[20] programmes. These courses are free of subject content and claim to develop particular Thinking Skills and attitudes to learning that can/will be transferred into other contexts. Instrumental Enrichment could also be placed in this category.

2 'Bolt-on' subject specific courses such as CASE and CAME. These courses again occur as 'packages' of lessons to be covered. They develop skills particular to the target subject but are not integrated into the general programme or scheme of work. They are seen as additional lessons, although teachers are often encouraged to use the techniques in other lessons for the subject.

3 Subject specific embedding where identified Thinking Skills and Strategies are developed within the overall scheme of work. Examples such as Thinking Through Geography demand no additional time but enhance pupils' Thinking Skills and their understanding of content.

Whole school embedding where Thinking Skills are planned and delivered across the curriculum. The ACTS (Activating Children's Thinking Skills) programme is an example of this approach.

In her report, McGuinness[8] identified three categories, merging 2 and 3 above. However, she was emphatic in stating what is of paramount importance in these approaches, and one with which we would agree: whichever model is adopted the strategies must be transferable out of that particular context. Again, the emphasis is firmly on the usefulness of the strategies that form Thinking for Learning.

To infuse or not

Swartz and Parks[18] describe the process by which Thinking Skills are taught through the content of various subject disciplines (i.e. 3 and 4 above) as *infusion*. They believe this approach to be more successful than the teaching of thinking in separate, content-free programmes.

Approaches to Teaching Thinking Skills

Teaching of
Thinking

| Direct teaching of Thinking
Skills outside of subject areas |

Teaching for
Thinking

| Uses methods to promote
thinking in subject contexts |

Infusion*

| Restructing lessons in subjects to
provide teaching of Thinking Skills |

* *Infusion* integrates the teaching of specific Thinking Skills into the content area of lessons,
so both thinking and the understanding of content benefit.

Infusion, as an approach to teaching Thinking Skills, combines subject content with skilful thinking that can be used in everyday lives to make good decisions and to solve problems effectively. They argue that the process of infusion is a natural way to structure the content of lessons. This assertion is based on the view that the curriculum is not just pieces of information that have some intrinsic value themselves, but can be considered as the data to help individuals grow into critical thinkers able to make judgements of their own.

According to Swartz and Parks there are three basic principles that support the infusion approach:

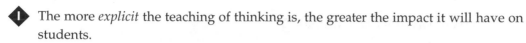

1 The more *explicit* the teaching of thinking is, the greater the impact it will have on students.

2 The more the classroom ethos promotes an atmosphere of *thoughtfulness* (reflection), the more open students will be to valuing good thinking.

3 The more the teaching of thinking is *integrated* into content instruction, the more students will think about what they are learning.

It could be argued by supporters of 'bolt-on' generic courses that the first two principles equally support their approach and that the third is just a matter of bridging what is learnt, so that it transfers to other areas of the curriculum and the learner's life. In fact, if the teaching of Thinking Skills is kept non-subject specific, then are the skills themselves not highlighted, clear of the confusion of subject content? Would their usefulness not then be *more* transferable, rather than dismissing, say, Odd One Out as a strategy used in RE?

Possibly. But this is surely a matter of effective teaching. The non-subject Thinking Skills course can be a useful addition to the curriculum, perhaps as a series of study skills lessons (especially early on in school) or to target a particular problem in learners, such as that for which the Instrumental Enrichment course was initially designed. The usefulness of the strategies taught here could be demonstrated for use outside that classroom. However, in the infused curriculum Odd One Out would not only have appeared in RE, but also in French and in English literature. Its use would have been experienced in a practical situation. The effective subject teacher will have drawn out what it is that the students have done; the learning will be made explicit. Applications for the strategies elsewhere will begin to appear. As has been reported to us, one boy asked a non-Thinking Skills teacher if he could use a Living Graph to complete his work, a transfer that he saw as relevant for that situation. Furthermore, how many times will the generic course need to be taught before a Thinking Skill is readily remembered in that 'vacuum'. And, if we are honest, how much curriculum time can be set aside? Is it really not better to infuse these skills into the curriculum and let the students reap the rewards already laid out?

Thinking skills in the National Curriculum

The Thinking Skills agenda cannot be seen any longer as an academic exercise. Statements in favour of a Thinking Skills agenda have been made recently by central figures in the continuing education debate.[21, 22] In the current National Curriculum, 'Curriculum 2000', all subjects are expected to develop Thinking Skills.

National Curriculum thinking skills

Information processing

Enables pupils to:

* locate and collect relevant information
* sort
* classify
* sequence
* compare and contrast
* analyse part/whole relationships

Reasoning

Enables pupils to:

* give reasons for opinions and actions
* draw inferences and make deductions
* use precise language to explain what they think
* make judgements and decisions informed by reasons or evidence

Enquiry

Enables pupils to:

* ask relevant questions
* pose and define problems
* plan what to do and how to do research
* predict outcomes and anticipate consequences
* test conclusions and improve ideas

Creative thinking

Enables pupils to:

* generate and extend ideas
* suggest hypothesis
* apply imagination
* look for alternative innovative outcomes

Evaluation

Enables pupils to:

* evaluate information
* judge the value of what they read, hear and do
* develop criteria for judging the value of their own and others' work and ideas
* have confidence in their judgements

At the time of writing, it is not clear how the government intends to pursue its aim of developing our ability to think and learn and there appears to be some confusion over this. The much talked about 'Transforming Teaching and Learning' agenda for Key Stage 3 seems to be in some turmoil. By the time this book is published, this issue may have been resolved. However, it seems no bad thing that there should be some confusion over this key area. If we also consider that most of what we actually know about the mechanics of the brain has only been learnt in the last five years,[23] then the last thing we need is a prescriptive national strategy telling us how to develop thinking in every classroom. A proper emphasis on research and development, with all parties encouraged to innovate and evaluate, is the only way that we will be able to establish a new ethos for learning in our schools. Schools and classroom teachers need to be at the centre of such research.

Accelerated Learning

Many of us will be familiar with the work of Alistair Smith and his Accelerated Learning Cycle.[24] For several years he has espoused the advantages to be gained from this approach to learning. Essentially, the term is used to describe practical approaches to teaching and learning that draw on current brain and educational research. It deals with issues such as self-esteem, preferred learning styles and pupil intelligences that together can help learners access and get the most from their education.

The cycle sets out a structured approach to teaching and learning that has been described in detail elsewhere.[7, 24]

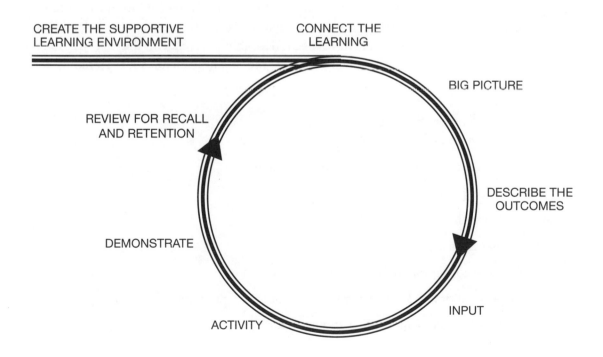

The Accelerated Learning Cycle

Because sections of the Thinking Skills movement draw upon some of the same research as that used in Accelerated Learning, we consider that the two share certain beliefs. For example, both discuss the idea that intelligence is modifiable, rather than fixed; that connections with existing knowledge need to be made; and that learning processes should be explained with a language for learning introduced. We accept that there are certain differences in emphases between the two, but what is important is that, at a practical level, they can complement one another.

There are Thinking Skills teachers throughout the country who relatively recently have been introduced to the techniques for Accelerating Learning. They have taken on board the benefits in much of what the brain research has presented them. However, what seems to have particularly struck a chord is what Accelerated Learning has to offer in terms of learning environment. This is twofold. First, there is the physical environment and how, for example, the education of 'visual learners' can be complemented by specific classroom display. Second, there is the effect that a safe, supportive learning environment can have on the individual. For reasons such as these we believe that Accelerated Learning provides a third environment: that as the host to infused Thinking Skills lessons, suitably informed by what we know about the learning brain, to take us forward into what we know as Thinking for Learning.

◆ Principles of thinking for learning

'Give a person a fish and you feed him for a day.
Teach him how to fish and you feed him for a lifetime.'

Chinese Proverb

Thinking Skills intervention strategies tend to have certain generic principles in common. Although the terminology may sometimes vary slightly from what is referred to in Accelerated Learning, we believe that these central tenets also help define what we have been describing. As such, the list we have compiled below forms the main principles of Thinking for Learning.

✔ Intelligence is modifiable

✔ Challenge and interest can lead to motivation

✔ Participation is valued

✔ Collaboration: learning with others

✔ Mediation is essential

✔ Promote conceptual understanding

✔ Metacognition: making learners think about their thinking

✔ Provide learners with explicit strategies for thinking

✔ Bridging for transfer.

Intelligence is modifiable

Intelligence has long been (and probably will continue to be) a source of controversy. For years it was assumed by many that there was a 'general intelligence'. Furthermore, a common view was that this was fixed and that it could be measured relatively simply. Increasingly, these views and the rationale behind them are being questioned, especially by those in education and psychology.

Reuven Feuerstein argued that it is more important to recognise and develop a person's potential for learning rather than to measure at any one point in time their apparent ability.[10] Similar thoughts occur when reading Howard Gardner's work on multiple intelligences.

> The IQ movement is blindly empirical. It is based simply on tests with some predictive power about success in school and, only marginally, on a theory of how the mind works. There is no view of process.[25]

Gardner looked at intelligence from a process perspective and found that the traditional view was only part of the whole picture. To date, he has identified eight and a half human intelligences (the half being one that needs further research) of which, he states, each individual has a unique combination. All of us have these intelligences to a greater or lesser degree depending on environment. Importantly for Thinking for Learning, Gardner, amongst others, believes that these intelligences are not fixed and that teachers can help develop them in a number of ways. To us, this vindicates what many teachers have been saying for years – that every pupil has their own strengths.

So, the human brain has capacities well in advance of those we are normally encouraged to develop in our young people. A Thinking for Learning approach aspires to capitalising upon this potential more effectively.

Challenge and interest can lead to motivation

Are you sometimes made to feel that if pupils are smiling, look happy in their work or seem to be enjoying themselves that learning cannot really be taking place? This view is less widely held now, but it once seemed endemic because 'that wasn't how it was when I was at school!' Many of us today realise that if lessons are interesting and enjoyable, learning is more likely to take place. Of course, lessons need to have structure, with the content being presented in effective ways that are also interesting, and this is where Thinking for Learning is useful.

Not only can an overall structure be provided, whether through the Accelerated Learning Cycle or one of the Thinking Skills approaches, but some of the strategies, such as 'Living Graphs' and 'Odd One Out', can lead to some real fun in the classroom. Very often these strategies lead to serious and thoughtful debate. But none of these is a panacea. They also require a supportive school and classroom environment and skilful teaching.

Activities should also be challenging without being stressful. Alleviating the stress is partly connected to the learning environment and partly to pupils' self-esteem. We will discuss both of these issues later in the book. For effective learning to take place in our schools, the pupil is best faced with high challenge and low stress. Thinking for Learning attempts to encourage such situations that stretch pupils' thinking beyond their existing comprehension and into what Vygotsky called that 'Zone of Proximal Development'. In CASE science this is described as the 'Zone of Cognitive Conflict'. By engaging pupils in conversation and encouraging them to strive for an appropriate solution, their interest and motivation can often be captured.

Participation is valued

This may seem a somewhat obvious principle, but it is surprising how little active participation occurs within some of the country's classrooms. Too often pupils are treated as empty vessels to be filled with the knowledge of the teacher. The result of this attitude is revealed in a recent study. Of 2600 interviewees aged between 14 and 16, a whole 56 per cent said they thought learning was copying from the board or a book, or listening in silence. Not much active participation there!

Thinking for Learning advocates the pupil as enquirer, thinker, hypothesiser, participator. In Philosophy for Children, for example, Matthew Lipman's 'Community of Enquiry', amongst other things, expects pupils to listen and build upon others' contributions. Emphasis is placed upon everyone thinking critically about these contributions, challenging assumptions, requesting clarification and assisting each other with drawing inferences from the discussions. Each individual's opinion is valued, never disparaged. The learners are all actively involved in creating an understanding of their chosen subject.

A by-product of this type of active participation is that it can increase motivation and behaviour. Our own observations and those of the many teachers now involved in various teaching strategies related to Thinking for Learning indicate that behaviour is often improved by the introduction of such lessons. By their nature, such activities are participatory, collaborative and interesting. When carefully structured and delivered with sufficient pace, there is much less room for misbehaviour and less boredom and passivity to encourage it. There has also been anecdotal evidence to suggest that the inclusiveness of such activities can raise the self-esteem of learners.

Collaboration: learning with others

Most pupils claim to enjoy working together, and enjoyment, as already discussed, is an important disposition for learning to take place. Being able to discuss their work and their understanding of it with peers helps pupils to establish their viewpoint and clarify their own understanding. Throughout the Accelerated Learning Cycle, the value of collaboration is celebrated in some of the activities for the pupils. At the 'demonstration' stage, for example, learners could explain to others what they have understood that lesson, share the results of an information search or discuss with a partner questions that might be used at the 'describe the outcomes' stage for another class taking the same lesson later. All will help the learner clarify the information for storage.

Paired and group work can be very effective but needs to be well structured and managed to avoid off-task activity.

Mediation is essential

Providing the learner with a stimulus but little structure for making sense of it rarely leads to progress in understanding. Professor John Edwards in Queensland, Australia discovered that pupils in very pupil-centred and resource-based classrooms often made disappointing progress. Whilst they were interested and motivated, without challenging interventions by the teacher their work often reverted to quite low-level copying or précising of stimulus material.

The pupils' reversion to their 'comfort zone', where little learning takes place, seems to accord with Feuerstein's belief that new material needs to be mediated if it is to be meaningfully understood.[10] This argument contradicts Piaget's assertion that children automatically progress to the formal operational stage of thought through interacting freely with stimuli. Feuerstein believed that human mediation of new information and experiences (e.g. through the mother or father) is needed in order to help shape children's perception of their world. He stated that Piaget's theory could not account for some of the disparities in abilities unless experiences were mediated. So, in educational terms, teachers need to mediate new information for pupils so that they can come to a better understanding of it and rise to the challenge rather than shrink back to their worksheets.

So:

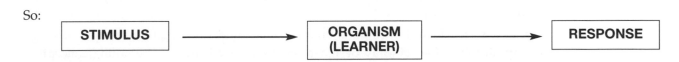

leads to an incomplete and unstructured understanding.

Whilst:

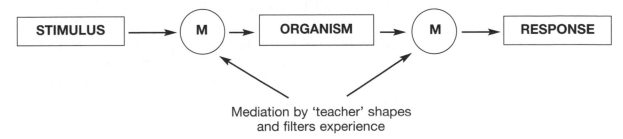

Mediation by 'teacher' shapes
and filters experience

leads to a more coherent and satisfying comprehension.

So, as teachers we are not only here to provide the content and resources, we are also here to *teach*: to interact with pupils, to challenge them, to support their learning, to question them carefully to uncover misconceptions and develop deeper understanding. Conventional whole class discussion rarely allows this to happen to any real degree.

Promote conceptual understanding

English Teachers have long vilified the traditional comprehension test. Its inadequacies are easily pointed out, as no apparent understanding of the material is needed to answer the questions. Take, for example, the following line from *Jabberwocky*:[26]

He took his vorpal sword in hand

How was the sword described? Easy enough. It is obviously an adjective, but what it means or what it might mean are entirely different, and more challenging, questions. Is it *bright, powerful, iron, useless?* It is only by looking at the context can we even begin to make an educated guess (and in the case of this poem, that is all it would be). The point here is that answering the question correctly does not necessarily denote full comprehension. The correct questions need to be asked and the learner's understanding checked.

The correct material also needs to be taught and presented in an accessible way. You only understand new information relative to that which you already understand. We do not develop our conceptual understanding of a subject by simply being told or reading about it.

At the University of Newcastle, David Leat has identified a small number of key 'foundation concepts' that are essential for a real understanding of geography. The Thinking Skills strategies developed by him and a group of teachers working with him are constructed so as to address these key concepts.[14] In other words, they are laying out the foundations on which they hope to build a fuller understanding of geography through their application of specifically designed tools for their learners. Promoting conceptual understanding of a subject goes to the core of teaching the content of a particular curriculum area.

Metacognition: making learners think about their thinking

In a rapidly changing world, knowing 'what' is only going to be of transient use to us because 'what' is likely to change before long. But knowing 'how', especially how to learn, is likely to be a valuable ability. To be able to learn we need to think about, and recognise, how we think and learn as individuals.

In their book *The Unfinished Revolution*, John Abbott and Terry Ryan state:

> Schools need a new focus on teaching practice that openly and continuously emphasises children's ability to understand their own thinking and learning. All this has to become more 'visible'.[2]

Such metacognition is at the heart of the Thinking for Learning approach. It is the conscious attempt by teachers to help pupils to think about their thinking and to recognise what they are doing as they learn and how these processes help. This might translate as the importance of talk, collaboration, kinesthetic activity or learned strategies, such as applying De Bono's PMI (Plus, Minus, Interesting) classification. When the strategies are accompanied by skilful mediation and de-briefing by the teacher, it can become the key to each learner's success and assist the much talked about 'lifelong learning' of such individuals.

Provide learners with explicit strategies for thinking

When we make learners think about their thinking we need to give them the strategies to use. Back in the 1970s, Edward de Bono was proposing that we equip pupils (and adults) with a set of relatively simple strategies for dealing with different situations. So we had PMI (Plus, Minus, Interesting), CAF (Consider All Factors), etc. More recently Top Ten Thinking Tactics has explored similar strategies for primary age pupils.

Through their use in the classroom, many pupils may learn to see the possible application of the strategies in other subjects. However, Thinking for Learning states that it is important that learners are made aware of the names of the strategies and how these processes work. They need to understand what works best for them and why. By the end of their schooling they should then be able to select strategies appropriate for themselves and the learning experience they find themselves faced with.

Bridging for transfer

As suggested above, the real measure of success for most learning is whether or not it 'transfers' into other contexts, especially into 'real life' situations (not that school is not very real for several years of our lives). Thinking for Learning attempts to consciously encourage this transfer by 'bridging'.

The process of bridging is a form of mediation that works by explicitly identifying the strategies used in the lesson and encouraging the learners to think about other situations where these might be used. For example, if a science lesson has just used a process involving the skill of classification, the learners might be required at the end of the lesson to think about what other subjects might gain from a similar process. Discussion might also focus upon what life would be like without any form of classification, drawing learners' attentions to its pervasiveness. It is important that bridging is planned for and structured, so that it does not deteriorate into an almost throwaway question at the end. If this occurs, the pupils may soon judge it as superfluous and a sign that the learning has finished.

When pupils are able to make these connections and use strategies and concepts in new situations within the same subject or in other subjects (or outside of school), then transfer is deemed to have taken place. The transfer can be identified as either 'near' (into similar situations in the same, or related subjects) or 'far' (into situations well removed from the present classroom or even the school). Skills used later in life have achieved a significant amount of 'far transfer'.

Of course, transfer demands a willingness to recognise and value the skills used in the classroom. This is much more likely in a context where the teacher models the use of such strategies and talks openly about them, as in many aspects of Thinking for Learning.

Go to page 153 for a practical example of transfer

Far transfer: investigating fact and opinion

In a Blyth Middle School pupils were introduced to a strategy investigating fact and opinion in Year 6 when looking at the expansion of a nearby pharmaceutical company and its impact on the environment. Later in the year pupils on the School Council were encouraged to use the same thinking strategy when proposals for a new uniform were being discussed (far transfer). In the opinion of some of the staff this helped to take some of the 'heat' out of the discussion.

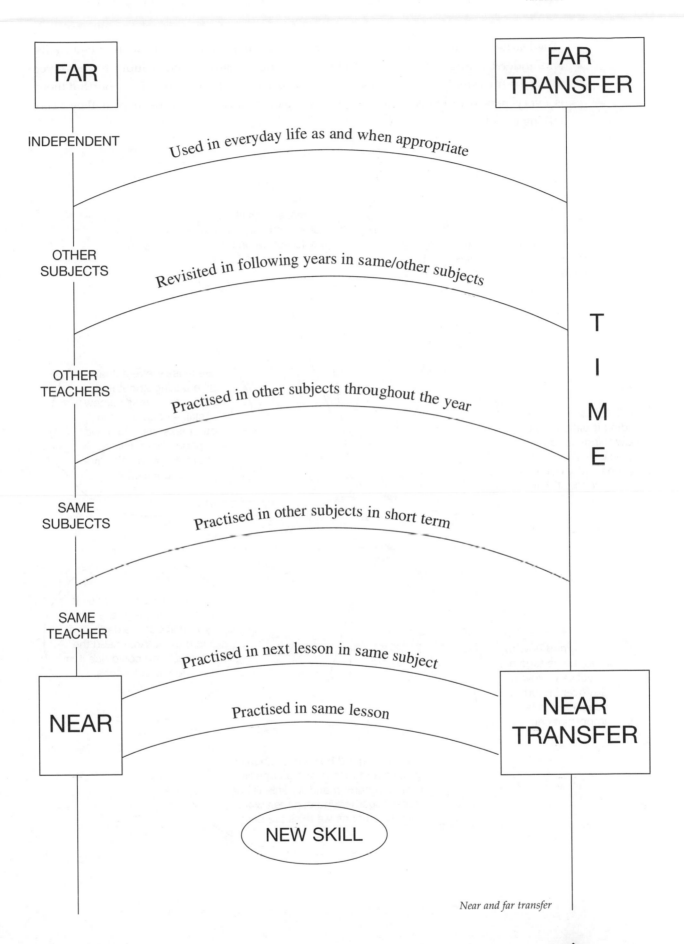

FAR

FAR
TRANSFER

INDEPENDENT

Used in everyday life as and when appropriate

OTHER
SUBJECTS

Revisited in following years in same/other subjects

OTHER
TEACHERS

Practised in other subjects throughout the year

T
I
M
E

SAME
SUBJECTS

Practised in other subjects in short term

SAME
TEACHER

Practised in next lesson in same subject

NEAR

Practised in same lesson

NEAR
TRANSFER

NEW SKILL

Near and far transfer

37

The learners quoted below are beginning to show an awareness of how their new skills and understandings will help them in these and other lessons. These pupils have not yet made the final steps of consciously using these skills in their lives outside school, but there is every reason to expect that they will develop this capacity, especially if they keep talking about it.

◆ Conclusion

In our work on Thinking For Learning it has become increasingly apparent that young people of any age can be taught to think more clearly, to express themselves and their thoughts more eloquently and to grow in self-esteem as a result. These attributes do not develop in all pupils simply through exposure to challenging and interesting tasks. Their thought processes and strategies for dealing with questions and problems need to be made explicit to them through skilful de-briefing about the process of the lesson, not only the content. These processes need to be given names so that pupils develop a thinking language and they need to be celebrated as valuable skills alongside more practical skills or academic knowledge and achievement. The principles outlined above may be used as a touchstone for all Thinking for Learning strategies advocated by us. In later chapters, their embedding within practical classroom activities will be apparent. However, these principles underlie every aspect of this book, as we attempt to carve out the ideal circumstances to evolve Thinking for Learning. The rationale behind some of these should grow increasingly clearer as we move on to discuss the focus of all our work: the learner.

Review

1 Choose five of the National Curriculum's Thinking Skills and devise tasks for two of your lessons that will enable the pupils to fulfil the relevant outcomes listed.

2 In what specific ways do you mediate the content of your lessons to make the information more accessible to your pupils?

3 Pupils often perform best when faced with high challenge and low stress. How do you ensure that your pupils are appropriately challenged without activities threatening their self-esteem?

4 Think of three examples of near transfer that were the result of your lessons. How did you encourage transfer to take place?

Thinking for learning activity: concept maps

Concept Maps are used to show and analyse relationships between certain factors. They require participants to think about and literally draw links between these factors, as seen on page 43.

What components do you think are needed to create an effective learning institution for children in the twenty-first century? These ideas are likely to be connected, so represent your ideas in a concept map, drawing out the links between them.

Thinking pupils

Preview

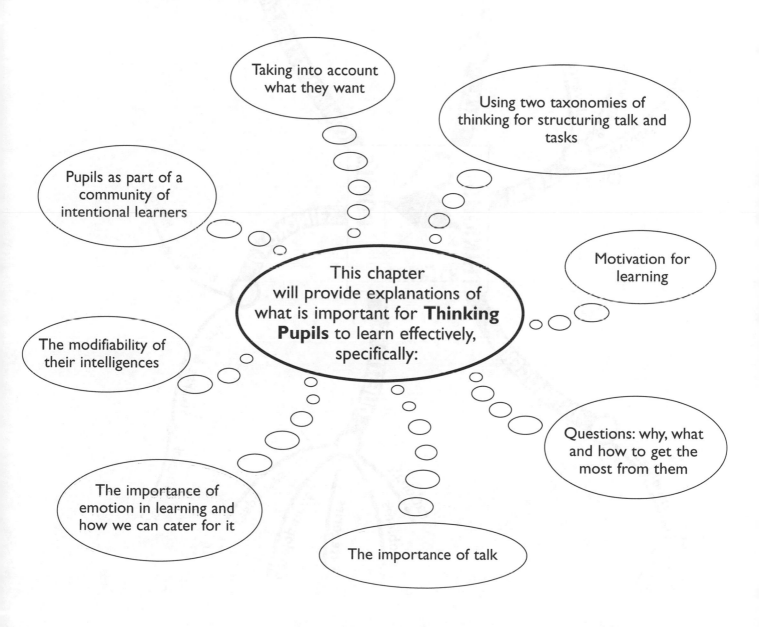

Taking into account what they want

Using two taxonomies of thinking for structuring talk and tasks

Pupils as part of a community of intentional learners

This chapter will provide explanations of what is important for **Thinking Pupils** to learn effectively, specifically:

Motivation for learning

The modifiability of their intelligences

Questions: why, what and how to get the most from them

The importance of emotion in learning and how we can cater for it

The importance of talk

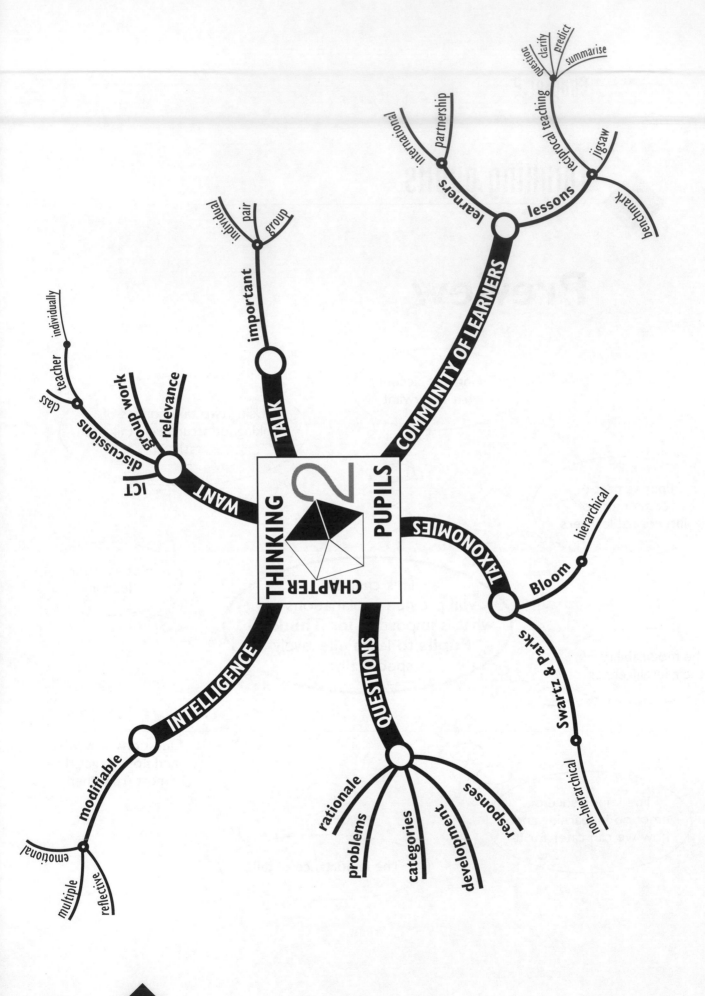

CHAPTER 2 THINKING

PUPILS

TALK
important
individual
pair
group

WANT
discussions
group work
relevance
ICT
teacher
class
individually

INTELLIGENCE
modifiable
emotional
multiple
reflective

QUESTIONS
rationale
problems
categories
development
responses

TAXONOMIES
Bloom
hierarchical
Swartz & Parks
non-hierarchical

COMMUNITY OF LEARNERS
learners
international
partnership
reciprocal teaching
question
clarify
predict
summarise
lessons
jigsaw
benchmark

THINKING FOR RAISING STANDARDS

EFFECTIVE LEARNERS

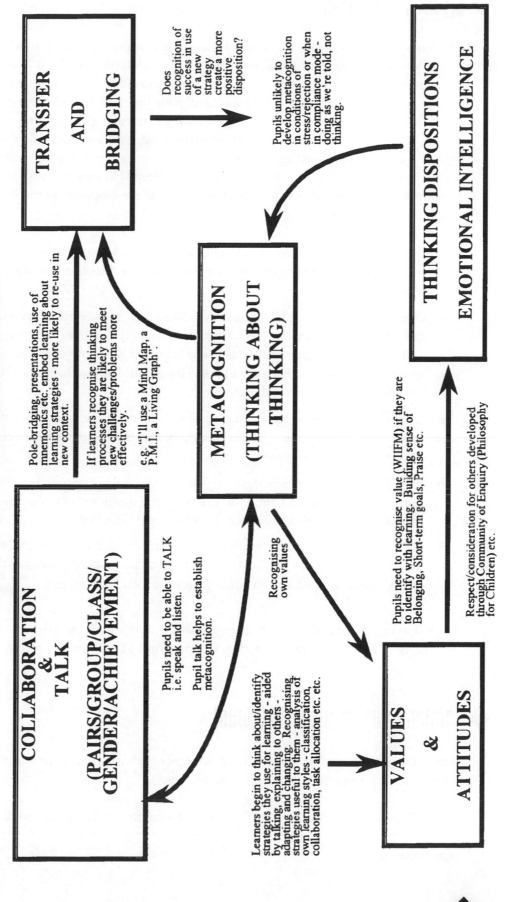

TRANSFER AND BRIDGING

Pole-bridging, presentations, use of mnemonics etc. embed learning about learning strategies - more likely to re-use in new context.

If learners recognise thinking processes they are likely to meet new challenges/problems more effectively.

e.g. "I'll use a Mind Map, a P.M.I., a Living Graph".

Does recognition of success in use of a new strategy create a more positive disposition?

Pupils unlikely to develop metacognition in conditions of stress/rejection or when in compliance mode - doing as we're told, not thinking.

METACOGNITION (THINKING ABOUT THINKING)

THINKING DISPOSITIONS EMOTIONAL INTELLIGENCE

COLLABORATION & TALK (PAIRS/GROUP/CLASS/GENDER/ACHIEVEMENT)

Pupils need to be able to TALK i.e. speak and listen.

Pupil talk helps to establish metacognition.

Recognising own values

Learners begin to think about/identify strategies they use for learning - aided by talking, explaining to others - adapting and changing. Recognising strategies useful to them - analysis of own learning styles - classification, collaboration, task allocation etc. etc.

Pupils need to recognise value (WIIFM) if they are to identify with learning. Building sense of Belonging, Short-term goals, Praise etc.

Respect/consideration for others developed through Community of Enquiry (Philosophy for Children) etc.

VALUES & ATTITUDES

◆ Effective learners

The concept map overleaf is the result of a working session of advisory staff and teachers that followed an Accelerated Learning training day in Northumberland. The complexity of the diagram illustrated to us how difficult it is to prioritise the key elements of effective learning or to create some sort of sequential map leading to a desired outcome. It is more likely that all the components shown in the diagram have to grow within the individual learner and each learning environment. Sometimes one will lead to another, or each will feed off the others so that all aspects gradually develop. Learning is not a simple scientific equation but a complex mixture of human interactions. However, to neglect any of the components shown would seem to us to preclude the development of the truly effective and autonomous learner. Why?

♣ Without a maturing Emotional Intelligence, which is appropriate for their age, pupils are unlikely to possess the disposition or the intention to think and to learn.

♣ Our level of Emotional Intelligence will affect, but is also affected by, our developing values and attitudes. Success and safety in the learning environment will breed more positive attitudes towards learning. Negative attitudes and value systems that dismiss learning will make it very difficult for learners to take advantage of their opportunities.

♣ Only through extensive discussion, talk and collaborative, socialising experiences can learners develop their understanding of themselves, the subject being studied and their attitudes towards it.

♣ As public talk and self-talk develop, learners build their own understanding of how they learn best and build self-esteem and a desire to learn. As this metacognition develops, so talk becomes more productive.

♣ Without a degree of metacognition it is difficult for pupils to consolidate what they have learned and to recognise and label those thinking processes that have helped them so that they can employ these processes elsewhere.

The following chapter deals with these issues in more detail but here we can see the continuing interdependence of these key components in the learning process.

◆ Thinking pupils: what they want

One of the greatest, and most underused, sources of information about effective learning is the experience and insight of pupils themselves.

A MORI poll conducted on behalf of the Campaign for Learning[27] indicated some mismatch between what pupils value as learning opportunities and what they often experience.

When asked what they would like to do more of to help them learn better and what they most often experience, the following were their most common responses:

WOULD LIKE TO DO MORE		DO MOST OFTEN IN CLASS	
1 Work on a computer	33%	1 Copy from board or book	56%
2 Work in small groups to solve problems	33%	2 Have class discussions	37%
3 Have class discussion	28%	3 Listen to teacher for long periods	37%
4 Talk about my work with a teacher	22%	4 Take notes whilst teacher talks	26%
5 Take notes whilst teacher talks	22%	5 Work in small groups to solve problems	25%
6 Learn things relating to the real world	18%	6 Spend time thinking quietly on own	22%
7 Be able to move around	17%	7 Talk about work with teacher	22%
8 Listen to background music	17%	8 Work on a computer	12%
9 Change activity when losing concentration	16%	9 Learn things relating to real world	11%
10 Have a drink of water when needed	14%	10 Create pictures or maps to remember	6%

Much of this is very positive. In response to other questions, pupils agreed (70 per cent) that teachers help them understand how they learn best. This suggests that many teachers may already be adopting methods connected to Thinking for Learning, as it is process that is alluded to here. What should be considered are the ways in which the teachers help their pupils learn better. This would give a clearer indication, for our purposes, about the practices to which they refer.

Some of the things learners most value are also common features of their lessons: having class discussions, taking notes from teacher talk, working in small groups to solve problems and talking about their work with a teacher. Less prominent is their most valued activity, work on a computer, although it does feature in 12 per cent of the responses and has undoubtedly increased over the past ten years.

More prolific use of ICT in the classroom would be beneficial. Instead of merely being used as wordprocessors to make that history essay more presentable (a valuable lower level skill in itself), the world of computing and communication now holds a myriad of possibilities. There is an increasing number of CD ROMs and interactive learning packages that assist pupils in content, as well as in helping them to develop their reasoning skills; the internet allows them to explore a wider world of knowledge; and networks allow pupils to work collaboratively across long distances. Although not a thinking skill, the use of ICT is nevertheless a transferable skill that is a useful tool in Thinking for Learning. It is also something to which pupils would like more access.

It was heartening to see many (22 per cent) spending time thinking. Again, what form this took is a question that needs addressing. Were the individuals working out set problems, exploring and testing hypotheses, reasoning mentally? Or were they daydreaming about their plans for the weekend? Were the tasks structured with a feedback session, allowing learners to share how conclusions were reached? Did bridging activities follow? The answer to the latter is possibly 'no'. Otherwise for those who said they learnt things relating to the real world, we might have expected the figure of 11 per cent to be higher.

Despite many positives, some of the pupils' desired activities barely feature in their experience. Being able to change activity when concentration is failing, using background music, drinking water and being able to move around are all recognised by both learners and neuroscientists as contributing to a change of physiology that may encourage more effective learning. All are advocated by practitioners of Accelerated Learning.

So much of what we do as teachers is valued by pupils and seen as useful to them. Where there is scope for change, pupils are an excellent source of information about which changes might be most effective. But there appears to be many who still passively listen to teachers talking for long periods and spend a lot of time copying.

◆ Keep talking

When we talk about the work in our own group we use real language. That helps us to understand what the teacher has said in school language.

Year 9 boy in science lesson

Piaget, Vygotsky, Feuerstein all emphasise the importance of talk in learning. On the whole they refer to talking together, not talking at – that is, talk as a way of building understanding, of correcting misconceptions, of mediating the learning experience.

There is still far too little purposeful and on-task talk in many classrooms and yet research shows that carefully planned and structured pupil talk enhances motivation and improves results. Most Thinking for Learning strategies are best used as group activities and certainly involve a lot of pupil talk. Experience suggests that it is often useful to move from the individual response to sharing thoughts in pairs and then to working in groups.

INDIVIDUALS have time to process information and to shape initial response.

PAIRS share initial thoughts, reform them, agree priorities and mediate understanding.

GROUPS increase debate, refine judgements, allocate tasks and responsibilities.

Some teachers reject fostering pupil talk as an activity because they feel it leads to too much off-task chatter and classroom management problems. Our experience with Thinking for Learning suggests that the opposite is the norm. When the task is clearly structured and the pupils motivated by the lead-in and understanding of the objectives, the teacher should be able to circulate and often oversee/hear fruitful discussion taking place.

With the grouping stage of any activity, students often instinctively flock into friendship groups, which can sometimes be a cause of concern for the teacher. Will the less motivated elements of the class cause uproar when together and will that quiet group of individuals in the corner spend time staring at the desk in front of them? Sometimes friendship groups seem to work in the pragmatic teacher's favour. There may be an attitude of trusting certain groups to 'get on with it' and keeping the challenging elements together and away from those who the teacher believes will remain on task. We do not believe this is necessarily what will happen, nor condone it, but advocate more positive reasons for allowing friends to form groups together. Often, individuals find it easier to discuss emotive topics with people they know and trust, they may only 'open up' their thoughts to their friends. This does not mean, however, that more effective topics should not be raised in other groupings, just that a supportive learning environment may need to be established first. We will discuss this in more detail later.

It may also be better to begin group work with friendship groupings to condition the class in the protocols of how you expect these lessons to progress. Other groupings may then be used for different purposes, depending upon the content and the desired outcomes. Certainly when away from peer group pressures, some individuals can feel the burden of conformity lifted and perform well.

The potential advantages for this type of collaboration in learning are enormous. In the 'real world' rarely do we sit and agonise over problems and decisions individually; instead we hold meetings, have committees, talk to friends over a coffee and take advice. Working and learning together is a social activity that can at the same time be productive for classroom learning, as well as preparing the individual for what is to come later 'outside' in society. It can promote understanding, respect for others' opinions, engender turn-taking and encourage a positive disposition towards learning.

◆ A Community of learners

Schools should be communities where students learn to learn. In this setting teachers should be models of intentional learning and self-motivated scholarship, both individual and collaborative.

Ann Brown and Joseph Campion [41]

Ann Brown and her colleagues in the USA argue that knowledge and understanding are not static states but are relative to the context in which they are studied. Learning takes place through participation in a cultural learning experience and it is distributed across the mind, the body, the activity itself and the cultural setting.

According to this theory of learning the contributions of all partners – teachers, learners and others – are important parts of the process. It is essential in this context that the learner brings a level of *intentionality* to the classroom. That is, that the learner actually wants to learn, not just to please, to comply or to 'succeed'. If we are honest, even many of our more successful students lack this element of 'intentionality'. They wish to succeed, and recognise that to do so they may need to be compliant, co-operative and attentive, *but* their intention is to succeed *not* to learn. In this state they often fail to see the point of collaborative work or discussion. 'Just tell me what to do and I'll get on with it on my own' is a not uncommon attitude.

In Brown's 'Community of Practice' however, this attitude is not enough. All members of the community contribute to the learning of all the others. Reciprocal teaching is an important element of this through 'jigsaw' techniques and 'learning groups'. In this situation all pupils will be able to extend their understanding within their own 'zone of proximal development' (Vygotsky) and succeed with the aid of support from teachers, peers and resources.

Features of the community of learners

Reciprocal teaching

The teacher and a group of students take turns leading discussion. The leader begins by asking a question and ends by summarising the gist of the discussion. (Usually based on a reading of a text.) During discussion the rest of the group seek clarification and make predictions. Thus reciprocal teaching situations involve:

- questioning
- clarification
- prediction
- summarising.

Initially the teacher must model this process until the pupils become comfortable with it.

Jigsaw method

Students are assigned part of a topic to investigate and learn and subsequently teach the rest of the group through reciprocal teaching.

Benchmark lessons

Where the teacher introduces a topic to be studied, finds out what the students already know and what they want to know. The 'Big Picture' of the whole unit and intended outcomes is described.

Importance of ritual

Rituals are important in any classroom. Below is an example of how Mike Fleetham, from Paulsgrove Primary School in Portsmouth, has trained his pupils into the ways of Thinking for Learning. Here he has used a 'Smart Board' to give his class the Big Picture at the beginning of the day. We can see from his use of terminology that they are familiar with the terms MI (Multiple Intelligence), VAK (visual, auditory and kinesthetic learning) and EQ (emotional quotient). He has dealt the students into their own learning by revealing process, already having illuminated how each individual learns best. For example, every class member knows their own balance of intelligences. They need to, as the teacher uses these to help teach numeracy and spelling.

The teacher has also incorporated an 'EQ Challenge', deliberately throwing in the competitive word to appeal to the boys in the class. This begins the day with an activity most young pupils enjoy, whilst reviewing what they know about reading other people's emotions from facial expressions. To become an emotionally intelligent child, this is an important skill.

Notice too the use of music in the classroom. Here it is being used to set the mood for work, but he also uses different pieces for other outcomes, such as the theme to *Hawaii 5-0* to encourage the pupils to clean the classroom in a set time.

Again, the class understands the meaning of the following display. WILF is an interesting way of telling the class the objectives of the lesson ('What I'm looking for...'). In this way, the pupils know what it is they are aiming to do. TIBs ('This is because…') allow them to see the relevance of what they are doing, why it is important for them to be able to give this their best effort.

WILF
I'm looking for you to know and use 2D shape words…
TIB
…because you'll need this language to help you think about shapes tomorrow.

For a Community of Practice to succeed, certain criteria have to be achieved in terms of a learning ethos. All these criteria apply to our Thinking for Learning lessons, which might well be described as Communities of Practice, or Communities of Enquiry.
For example:

1 Individual responsibility and communal sharing.

2 Mutual respect between students and adults.

3 The valuing of discourse – discussion, questioning, critical analysis.

4 Ritual. Practices that are fair and consistent so that pupils easily recognise them and are at ease with terms such as Jigsawing, Reciprocal Teaching, Benchmark Lessons – or in Thinking for Learning it might be Pair and Share, Odd One Out, Classification, Check and Change (from Top Ten Thinking Tactics), and so on.

◆ Taxonomies of thinking

Using Bloom's taxonomy for structuring tasks

Another useful tool for structuring the talk and its situations is Bloom's Taxonomy of Thinking,[28] which underpinned many of the curricular developments of the 1960s and 1970s. Geography for the Young School Leaver (GYSL) and Nuffield Science both used this hierarchical theory of thinking to structure learning activities.

Bloom called his work a 'taxonomy' because he believed it to be a system classifying the levels of thinking, and it has much to offer the teacher when organising learning experiences. However, the theory has often been misinterpreted and misused under the assumption that young pupils, or those labelled as 'less able', can only deal with the first one or two, maybe three, rungs on the ladder. Thinking, though, is much more complex than this.

Bloom argued that thinking can be considered as developing from very simple thinking, where little understanding is shown but some knowledge is retained, to a highly complex activity involving the synthesis of many pieces of evidence so that a full understanding of an idea is attained. Most of our everyday thinking could be categorised as sitting somewhere along this continuum. Whilst our capacity to utilise highly complex thinking undoubtedly expands as we mature, we believe that it is a misinterpretation of Bloom to suggest that young children cannot analyse, evaluate or synthesise. Indeed they are involved in these processes from a very early age, as when they are assimilating the world around them, for example.

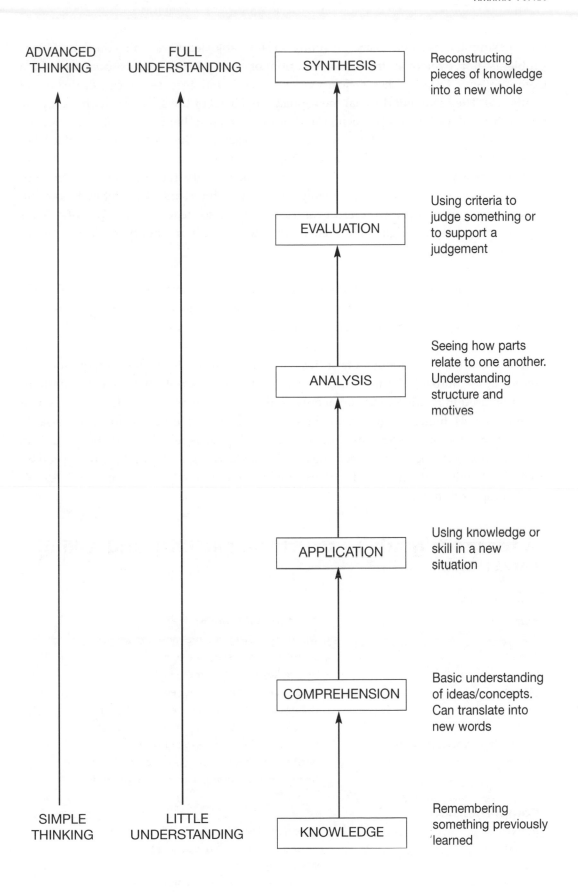

ADVANCED
THINKING

FULL
UNDERSTANDING

SYNTHESIS

Reconstructing
pieces of knowledge
into a new whole

EVALUATION

Using criteria to
judge something or
to support a
judgement

ANALYSIS

Seeing how parts
relate to one another.
Understanding
structure and
motives

APPLICATION

Using knowledge or
skill in a new
situation

COMPREHENSION

Basic understanding
of ideas/concepts.
Can translate into
new words

SIMPLE
THINKING

LITTLE
UNDERSTANDING

KNOWLEDGE

Remembering
something previously
learned

Giving simple repetitive tasks to young or less able learners will compound their problems not overcome them. Observation of very young pupils operating in a Community of Enquiry shows clear evidence that 5 and 6-year-olds can evaluate and synthesise. They may not do so at the sophisticated level of the sixth former but they are beginning to develop these capacities and need to practise them, not wait until they are old enough. Mediating activities will assist them to achieve this. A Middle School teacher once told us that he did not ask any meaningful questions to children below the age of 12 because it was well known that 'children can't think in an abstract way until they're 11 or 12'. A good example of how a very simplistic view of the work of Piaget or Bloom can lower expectations. It is a wonderful contrast to this to see teachers of pupils of all ages stimulating and challenging children's thinking through a variety of Thinking for Learning approaches.

What we would hope as we teach pupils, utilising Bloom's taxonomy, would be that the sophistication and complexity of pupils' thinking would develop as they practise and adopt the strategies for more effective thinking.

In relation to talk, one adaptation of the taxonomy is to use it for devising questions to guide pupils' thinking. To this end, the table below draws out what kind of questions might be used in relation to the taxonomy. Activities can be developed from it according to ability levels, though it must again be stressed that less able pupils do not necessarily work at the bottom whilst others operate at the higher levels. Instead they could do differentiated work upon the same rung as the other learners, each pupil operating at their own 'depth' within the level and with extension activities to expand more able children's more complex thinking.

A teacher's guide to structuring activity and asking questions

Knowledge

Activities	Questions for Learning
Tell	Which three things are the most important?
Recite	Describe them to someone else.
List	List the key characters in the book.
Memorise	Write your list, turn it over, repeat it.
Remember	Write your list, turn it over, repeat it, try again.
Find	Look for and list the ingredients needed.
Summarise in your own words	List five key things and explain each.
Locate	Where in the book would you find...?
Name	Name as many characters as you can; go for five.

Comprehension

Activities	Questions for Learning
Restate	What do you think is happening here?
Explain	What is significant?
Give examples of	Can you think of any other similarities?
Summarise	What do you consider essential?

Translate	What might this mean?
Edit	Using the cut and paste facility can you...?
Draw	What three things are the most important?

Application

Activities	Questions for Learning
Demonstrate	Plan and deliver a presentation to...
Based on what you know	What is most significant for your chosen audience?
Model	How can you best demonstrate your understanding?

Analysis

Activities	Questions for Learning
Investigate	What information is needed? Where will you get it?
Classify	Organise the data using a flow chart/concept map.
Categorise	List the data in categories for a given audience.
Compare and contrast	List arguments for and against. Compare them.
Relevant and irrelevant	Choose a target audience. List relevancies and irrelevancies for them.
Facts and opinions	Separate into fact and opinion using a Venn diagram.
Fallacies	What assumptions are being made? Why?

Evaluation

Activities	Questions for Learning
Prioritise	Reorder with a justification.
Rate	Design a mechanism to evaluate the importance of...
Grade	Devise a hierarchy of significance.
Critique	Discuss the relative merits in relation to...
Judge	Following your critique, say which is better and why.
Recommend	What is the best option? Why? List five reasons.

Synthesis

Activities	Questions for Learning
Create	Provide a portfolio of evidence showing your case for...
Compose	Taking the theme of stillness, produce three pieces for the piano.
Invent	You need an effective labour-saving device for...
Construct	Using appropriate materials based on your research, produce...
Combine	Your audience of fund managers need a multi-media presentation...
Forecast	Using all the evidence available...
Formulate	As a result of the analysis of data, give the cost-effective solution to...
Argue the case for	Listen to the evidence, summarise, critique, choose and recommend.
Predict	Based on the evidence and your intuitive feelings, say what you think is likely to...
Imagine	Being as unconventional as you like, try to envisage a ...

Alistair Smith [7]

Swartz and Parks' taxonomy: a different view

As mentioned earlier, Bloom's taxonomy was open to misinterpretation, partly due we feel to its linear presentation. Working in primary education in the USA in the 1980s and 1990s, Swartz and Parks developed a non-hierarchical analysis of Thinking Skills that identifies different types of applications for thinking.

Swartz and Parks' alternative taxonomy identifies a range of characteristic functions of thinking. All these can be introduced at an early stage in a child's development and improved over a period of time by helping the learner to develop conscious strategies for thinking and by ensuring that opportunities for those types of thinking are built into the curriculum at regular intervals.

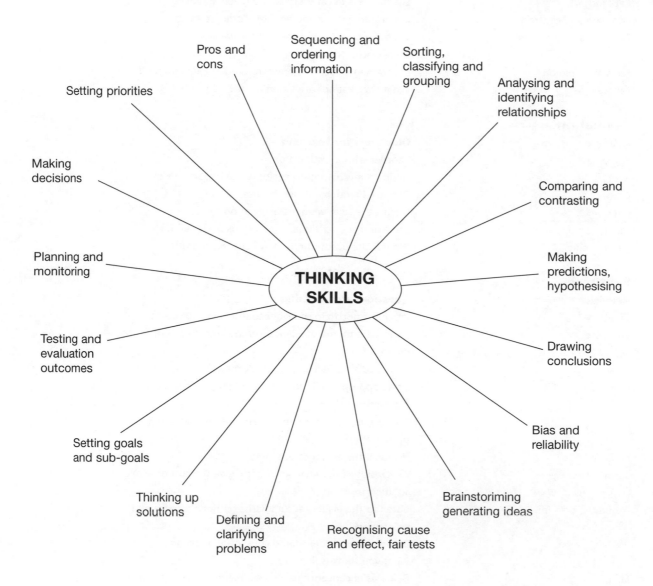

When looking at this collection, we recognise many aspects of our everyday lives as teachers or managers of learning. How else do we devise effective lesson plans, schemes of work or school development plans?

Over the page are examples of the types of questions that might be used to encourage the requisite thinking functions outlined opposite. We have compiled these questions in part from those suggested by Swartz and Parks.[18]

When translated into practical examples it is easier to see the possibilities for making all thinking functions available to every pupil, whatever their age or ability. With 'comparing and contrasting', for example, differentiation could be through the subject material or through outcome when using appropriate mediation to introduce the content. Like Bloom, Swartz and Parks have suggested a taxonomy for thinking that can be practical in its application and inclusive at the same time.

◆ The importance of questions

Why ask them?

Questioning comes in various forms, not just in those used to structure activities. Probably the most common classroom activity seen in England is a sea of hands going up (or not) in response to questions being asked by the teacher. Whilst this is often a good way of warming up pupils for the rest of the lesson, as teachers we should ask ourselves why we concentrate quite so much on this technique. It is so embedded in our practice, and encouraged by recent national trends, that most of us never stop to think about whether we perhaps overuse whole class questioning. Certainly there are some problems inherent in this type of questioning:

* Inevitably only one (of 30+) pupils can respond at once.

* It is possible for some pupils to be totally passive and inactive.

* If it lasts too long, such whole class activity leads to unrest and disruption as some pupils lose concentration.

* Pupils learn particular avoidance techniques to suit the teacher; for example, sitting on the periphery (research shows that pupils closest to the teacher get most attention), not putting your hand up, putting your hand up (when you know the teacher always picks out those with their hands down) or 'forgetting' when asked.

We need to decide why we are asking questions and then choose appropriate styles of question.

Setting priorities
- What things do you need to do?
- Why do they need prioritising?
- Can any be left until another day?
- Which of those remaining need to be done soon to avoid a possible problem?
- Which, then, are the most important?

Pros and cons
- What are the positives and what are the negatives of the discussion?
- How does this make you feel towards the proposal?
- Can any of these pros or cons be resolved to sway you one way or the other?

Making decisions
- What is this decision for?
- What are your options?
- What are the consequences of each option?
- How important are the consequences?
- What is the best option in view of the consequences?

Planning and monitoring
- What is it that you need to achieve?
- What must be considered when planning to achieve it?
- What are your options to achieve this aim?
- Which options take into account the considerations?
- How can you fit them together to reach your aim?
- How will you know if it is working?

Testing and evaluating outcomes
- What are the results of your proposal?
- Is the outcome as you expected, better or worse?
- How might the outcome be improved?
- How will you know?

Setting goals and sub-goals
- What do you want to achieve?
- What do you need to do to be able to achieve this goal?
- How are these things best accomplished?
- When will you know you have achieved your goal?

Thinking up solutions
- What is it that you need to be able to do?
- What is stopping you?
- What are your options?
- What are the consequences of these options?
- Which will best help you to do what you need to?

Defining and clarifying problems
- Why will your idea not work?
- Has everything been done as you intended it to be?
- Was there a flaw in your reasoning?
- What are your options?

**TH
S**

quencing/ordering ormation
- Why do you want to order them?
- What is the best way to do this?
- What do you need to know about each one so that they can be arranged?
- Where does each one fit?

Sorting, classifying and grouping
- What features do the given items possess?
- What classifications do these features suggest?
- Why do you want to classify these items?
- What way of classifying them best serves this purpose?
- Which items fall into this category?

Analysing and identifying relationships
- What smaller things make up the whole?
- For each of these parts, what would happen to the whole if it were missing?
- What is the function of the part?

Comparing and contrasting
- How are these items similar?
- How are they different?
- Which similarities and differences seem significant?
- What pattern does this suggest to you?
- What conclusion can you draw from the significant similarities and differences?

Making predictions, hypothesising
- What might happen?
- What evidence indicates this?
- Based on the evidence, is the prediction likely or not?

Drawing conclusions
- What is the source trying to convince you of?
- How are they trying to do this?
- Does the language they use influence you in any way?
- What reasons do they provide for their opinion?
- Is there any evidence for this?
- What conclusion do you reach about what the source is saying?

Bias and reliability
To find out whether a source is reliable or not, ask:
- Do they know the subject?
- Have they found out from someone else who is reliable?
- Have they found out by careful research?
- Have they a reason for wanting you to believe them?
- Are they known and trusted by others?
- Does anyone else think the same as them?

Recognising cause and effect
- What are the possible causes of the event in question?
- What evidence would support or oppose these possibilities?
- What evidence do you already have that is relevant to determining what caused the event?
- Which is the most likely possibility, based on the evidence?

Brainstorming, generating ideas
- What do you need these ideas for?
- How do you best generate ideas?
- What are the most obvious ideas?
- Are there any unusual possibilities?

After Swartz and Parks [18]

NG
S

57

So when do questions help learning?

? Questions can help connect existing knowledge to new contexts.

? Questions can help pupils review and recall what they have learned.

? Reflective, open questions can model how experienced learners seek new meanings.

? Questions can reveal variations in understanding and knowledge and can expose misconceptions.

? Questions can help pupils to organise their unsorted knowledge and to structure their lines of thought.

? Questions can establish the focus for the lesson or re-align pupil thinking with the objectives of the lesson.

? Open questions can stimulate discussion and debate, enabling pupils to express their own views and opinions and to query and challenge the opinions and values of their peers.

? Questions can give pupils who have difficulty with writing an opportunity to participate and show what they know orally.

What sort of questions?

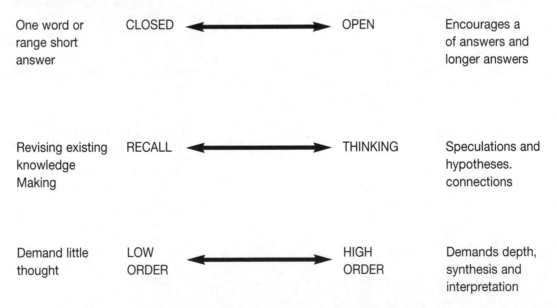

One word or range short answer	CLOSED ⟷ OPEN	Encourages a of answers and longer answers
Revising existing knowledge Making	RECALL ⟷ THINKING	Speculations and hypotheses. connections
Demand little thought	LOW ORDER ⟷ HIGH ORDER	Demands depth, synthesis and interpretation

Research indicates the average length of pupil response as two seconds and a preponderance of low order, closed and recall questions, whilst open and pseudo-open questions can cause stress and confusion if they are too complex, not contextualised or not posed in a reflective and open manner.

Some common problems with questions

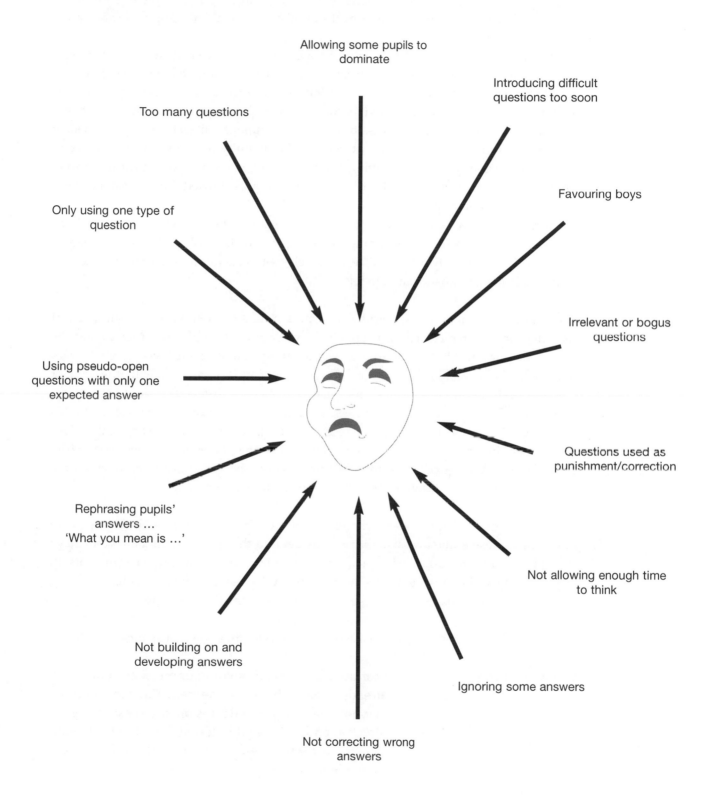

Allowing some pupils to dominate

Introducing difficult questions too soon

Too many questions

Favouring boys

Only using one type of question

Irrelevant or bogus questions

Using pseudo-open questions with only one expected answer

Questions used as punishment/correction

Rephrasing pupils' answers …
'What you mean is …'

Not allowing enough time to think

Not building on and developing answers

Ignoring some answers

Not correcting wrong answers

Questions for thinking

Too many closed or obscure questions will actually inhibit pupil response and hinder thinking. Skilful questioning will engage the pupils' interest and develop a line of enquiry.

The Community of Enquiry approach (see page 110) is an excellent way of generating questions, making sure that pupils participate fully in lessons and that they are answering questions they have shown an interest in. Whilst this technique is most usually associated with Philosophy for Children and questions are explored in a neutral context, the approach has also been used successfully in more traditional subjects. At Blyth Tynedale High School (now Blyth Community College) a Community of Enquiry was set up with three Year 9 classes that were studying population movement as part of their geography course. The classes were set by ability. In all classes pupils showed improvement in their abilities to formulate questions and to discuss them. Whilst the normal school lesson offers relatively few opportunities for original thinking, these lessons encouraged the pupils to explore their understanding of the topic and its implications for the people involved. Thus the study was made 'real' and relevant to the pupils, rather than a pseudo-academic study of statistics and models.

Pupils in the lowest ability set produced some excellent written work that showed real empathy for the predicament of people involved in migration between Mexico and the USA. They found discussion in the whole group difficult but were able to talk constructively in pairs. The middle ability group coped very well with the idea of philosophical questions. Students formulated questions, listened to each other and generally responded well to someone else's comments. The most able pupils took to this method easily and generated lots of questions. This group were the most critical of their own viewpoints and several changed their minds after listening to their peers. The students in all three groups felt that they understood and remembered more about the topic of migration as a result of their philosophical discussions.

This experience corresponds with the results of other attempts in schools. If pupils are setted, then those in the lowest ability groups can find the approach difficult – they have lots of ideas but often lack the language to communicate any sophisticated arguments. In mixed ability groupings pupils are helped greatly by having more articulate learning partners who can assist them in constructing and justifying their arguments.

Other well-documented methods to help pupils develop their own questions include:

Brainstorming   Best used as a way of building upon what pupils already know or have experienced. This can be done in whole class or group discussion and is especially effective and inclusive if initiated from the individual to pairs. The whole process should not last for more than a few minutes.

Transformation	Starting with descriptions or statements and changing these into questions by adding 'why, what, when, who, how, where?' For example: a) The Vikings sailed across the North Sea = 'Why did the Vikings sail across the North Sea?' b) The Nissan factory was built close to Sunderland = 'Why was the Nissan factory built close to Sunderland?' Younger pupils find this process difficult at first but soon become adept at it.
Question Captions	Using photographs, pictures, artefacts, etc. pupils ask questions about what is happening etc.

◆ Managing pupils' responses to questions

Processing time

When someone asks us a question we often need some time to think about our answer before giving it. We find it ironic that, in a learning environment, time for thinking can sometimes be overlooked in order to extract a response. This usually happens in one of two ways: it can be interrupted by our peers who want to answer first, or by a teacher who is impatient for an answer and does not want silence in case it encourages disruption. But teachers do need to give pupils time to:

☆ hear the question

☆ assimilate the question and relate it to existing knowledge

☆ formulate their response

☆ surface their response through language.[7]

Open-ended questions may well need ten to twenty seconds for pupils to formulate and offer a response. It could be a good idea to insist on ten seconds thinking time before accepting any answers.

Processing strategies

To make sure that *all* pupils are participating and thinking about a response to a question the following techniques can be used instead of asking for 'hands up'.

Timed Challenge	Can you think of three reasons in two minutes for...? (appropriate background music will help concentration and dull silence.)

61

Numbered Challenge	Can you think of three things to do with…/five reasons for…/seven different…? Research shows that all pupils respond better to a specified number of factors. Boys benefit most and respond well to such challenges.
Structured Challenge	Individuals think of one or more responses. Pairs share their answers. Pairs join up as groups of four and pool their responses. Groups report back to whole class.
Snowball Challenge	Similar to above but timed and to music; for example, remember one thing about x in ten seconds – on the bell/when the music stops swap with a neighbour to make two things – on cue swap with someone else to make four – to eight, etc.
Post-it Challenge	You have two minutes to write on the post-it three things you remember about x. Then I'll ask you to file up to the front and stick your post-it on the board.[7]

All the above share the characteristics:

- ♠ They don't require hands-up.
- ♠ All pupils are involved.
- ♠ There is challenge without stress.

Go to page 118 for practical strategies to encourage talk

Pupils will soon become used to such techniques and will begin to appreciate the benefits to their education. After all, there are few of us who cannot remember groaning in our own schooldays when the same people answered the teacher's questions time and again. If we are to recognise talk and questioning as vital to the classroom, then we must adopt such strategies to structure their use and make them accessible for all.

◆ Intelligence

It is not the intention of this book to indulge in an argument about the nature of intelligence. We have already outlined some of the main issues in Chapter 1 (see page 31). However, if we are to discuss learners, then we must return briefly to the subject and rehearse a few ideas here to describe how these have affected the development of the Thinking for Learning initiative.

Much work in schools, particularly in assessment and examination procedures, is still based on an acceptance that intelligence is a fixed commodity that can be measured. A liberal interpretation of this view accepts that each individual has the capacity to develop their intelligence to a certain level and that good teaching will enable the student to reach something like their optimum level. This view accepts that some pupils will do well whilst others will fall by the wayside and that this is entirely natural. This type of thinking reflects the views of the nineteenth-century behaviourist Francis Galton, who believed that intelligence was determined by nature, static and measurable. It is ironic that IQ tests seem to reflect this view and yet the one most commonly used in Western society was devised by a French psychologist, Alfred Binet, who believed that education and learning could actually improve a person's intelligence.

Teachers involved in Thinking for Learning would endorse the view that intelligence is by no means fixed, that we all possess a brain capable of immeasurably greater things than normally expected of it and that our individual capabilities are constantly changing and can be enhanced through creative teaching and learning.

Some views on intelligence

Reflective intelligence (David Perkins[52])

Perkins identifies three components of intelligence:

1 Fixed neurological intelligence that can be measured by IQ tests.

2 Specialised knowledge and experience learned over time.

3 Reflective intelligence about oneself and mental habits of mind.

It is this latter 'thoughtful intelligence' that Perkins argues is particularly necessary in the twenty-first century and that can best be developed to increase our intellect. This kind of intelligence helps us to make wise personal choices, to solve challenging problems, to find creative ideas and to learn complex topics in new contexts. However, he also argues that traditional schooling offers few opportunities to develop this reflective intelligence and that successful members of society develop it in their personal or home lives as opposed to in schools. Within Thinking for Learning we would argue that more opportunities arise to develop this component through the very nature of the strategies we use.

Multiple Intelligences (Howard Gardner)

It is very important that a teacher takes individual differences amongst kids very seriously. We know that people truly understand something when they can represent the knowledge in more than one way.

Howard Gardner [25]

Howard Gardner is a senior academic at Harvard University who since the early 1980s has developed his theory of Multiple Intelligence that has begun to have a major impact in some of our schools.

Gardner argues against the notion of a fixed, measurable Intelligence Quotient (IQ). In its place he argues that there are many ways in which we all develop. Initially Gardner identified seven types of intelligence and you may encounter many references to 'seven kinds of smart'. Recently, however, he has added another and others are under review.

There are critics of Gardner's work and some people have problems identifying with all the defined intelligences. What seems to us to be the fundamental and valuable message for Thinking for Learning is not a strict adherence to a set of seven, eight or nine intelligences, but an acceptance that we are all unique. We show our intelligences in different ways and at different times and that we all have the capacity to become 'more intelligent' in each area.

◆ Emotional Intelligence

What is it?

The old paradigm idealised reason as free of emotion. The new paradigm urges harmony of head and heart. To do well in life we must first understand more exactly what it means to use our emotions intelligently.

Goleman [29]

Academic intelligence has little to do with emotional life. If it did, why would Jason, a star pupil, have stabbed his physics teacher because he failed to get an A grade in one test? How could it be that some of the most highly educated and sophisticated European elite became responsible for the Holocaust?

Emotional Intelligence is a relatively new concept. Much of the thinking about it has been summarised in Daniel Goleman's fascinating best-selling book *Emotional Intelligence: Why It Can Matter More Than IQ*.[29] In this book Goleman argues that thinking and academic success are of little use to us without a well developed Emotional Intelligence – an understanding of and control over our feelings and emotions. Using case studies and drawing evidence from brain research, Goleman develops a convincing argument about the important effects of anger, sadness, fear and so on, in many aspects of our lives.

Without emotional learning our rational thinking becomes anything but rational. Patients with damage to areas of the brain connected to the emotions can become very poor decision-makers. They seem unable to predict the consequences of their decisions, particularly with regard to the reactions of other people. It seems that when we are faced with decisions in life, our emotional learning enables us to discount certain options and highlight others as likely to result in the outcome we desire. Without it we make 'rational' decisions that may result in unplanned for and disastrous consequences.

Why is Emotional Intelligence important for learning?

Our ability to learn most effectively depends upon our capacity for attaining what Goleman calls a state of 'flow'. In a state of flow our rational and emotional brains achieve balance. We are learning well and enjoying it! In this state many learners achieve more than they or others would have expected – athletes talk about being in 'the zone', artists speak of 'losing themselves' in their work. In our most successful lessons we observe pupils who become so involved that they are temporarily absorbed. To achieve this state in lessons we need to plan the activities well, but the pupils must also be able to take advantage of this.

'Reason must have an adequate emotional base for education to perform its function.'

Plato

Emotionally intelligent pupils of all abilities can cope with activities that are too simple or too difficult. They can recognise and control their own emotions. It seems to be the case that pupils who handle upsets, listen better, control impulses and feel responsible for themselves do better in examinations. This is an important message for schools where pupils underachieve: deal with their emotional, as well as their academic, well-being and the rewards are manifold. Pupils lacking Emotional Intelligence are often low achievers. They quickly become bored or over-anxious and then look for success and attention elsewhere – perhaps in the approval of their peers for their disruptive or 'clever' behaviour.

Can we teach Emotional Intelligence?

Pupils' attitudes and behaviours are shaped by emotional experiences in their lives. These can be difficult to modify through instruction or debate as they are usually deeply entrenched and often difficult to elucidate. Our most successful schools, however, undoubtedly include an element of education for Emotional Intelligence in their curriculum, whether consciously or not. These schools tend to recognise and accommodate different learning styles, celebrate success of all kinds and model constructive relationships. A positive ethos can do a great deal for pupils' self-esteem, a vital element of Emotional Intelligence. Also, the need for talk is again important. Through the discussion of philosophical issues in P4C, for example, deeply buried beliefs and attitudes can rise to the surface, allowing the speaker and others to question these in a 'safe' environment. As James Park,[30] director of a campaign for emotional literacy, points out, P4C and other structures for collaborative talk in a supportive environment can be a useful method for developing emotional literacy in PSHE, rather than more traditional instruction.

Alistair Smith's writing on Accelerated Learning includes references to what he calls the 'BASICS' model for pupil achievements (see pages 71 and 72).[7,24] This attention to fostering a sense of belonging, aspiration, success, identity, challenge and safety for all pupils again promotes Emotional Intelligence.

In some of our schools efforts are now being made to help pupils recognise their own types of intelligence by using Howard Gardner's Multiple Intelligences. By identifying, celebrating and building on the particular attributes of pupils, we can help strengthen their self-esteem and self-confidence. Thus they are more likely to enter that state of 'flow' in their learning and become confident enough to tackle their weaker areas.

For most of us our level of Emotional Intelligence is learned in the earliest years of our lives in response to the behaviours modelled by our parents and other significant people. Can schools do anything to redress the deficiencies in Emotional Intelligence displayed by some pupils? Intervention programmes in several schools suggest the answer is yes!

The *social* and *emotional* results of such learning are listed by Goleman[29] as:

* Improved ability to recognise and name own emotions.

* Better understanding of what causes our feelings.

* Ability to differentiate between feelings and actions.

* Better management of anger.

* Fewer verbal and physical assaults.

* Fewer suspensions and exclusions.

* More positive feelings.

* Less loneliness.

* More responsible, less impulsive behaviour.

* Improved test scores.

* Improved empathy.

* Better listening skills.

* More sharing and co-operation.

* More democratic behaviour.

Skills supporting Emotional Intelligence

∗ 'Self-talk' (inner dialogue) and self-awareness

∗ Recognising social cues (reactions of others)

∗ Problem-solving/decision-making applied to feelings

∗ Understanding other perspectives

∗ Positive attitude to life

∗ Non-verbal behaviours (eye contact, gestures, etc.)

∗ Verbal behaviours (listening, positive responses, assertiveness)

How do we achieve this?

So if the evidence shows us very strongly that it is possible to influence pupils' Emotional Intelligence, their self-esteem and ability to know themselves better, then how can we go about doing this in our schools? The experiences of individual teachers and schools in Northumberland support the view that the following approaches can all help.

♣ Pay attention to Emotional Intelligences in PSHE programmes, using P4C for example.

♣ Analyse and celebrate Multiple Intelligences. All pupils have something to offer.

♣ Adopt the BASICS model for your classroom.

♣ Develop Thinking for Learning strategies that promote reflection and analysis. For example:

　　♠ SOCS (Situation, Options, Consequences, Solution) to help analyse the consequences of actions and resolve issues more effectively. Pupils are encouraged to confront real-life situations and emotions to help to remove the compulsion from their thinking.

　　♠ ACTS (Activating Children's Thinking Skills), STSC (Somerset Thinking Skills Course) and Top Ten Thinking Tactics can all contribute to more analytical and less impulsive approaches to emotional responses.

The Discovery project

Discovery is a unique three-year project funded by Portsmouth City Education Department. It aims to develop and improve the Emotional Intelligence of individuals in the Paulsgrove cluster of schools. What is different about this programme, though, is that rather than just focusing on specific groups, it has adopted a more holistic approach by encompassing everybody in the school. This means that pupils, teachers, dinner ladies, heads, governors – everybody – is offered practical strategies for developing their potential through understanding themselves and by managing their emotions better. Measurable outcomes should include reduced incidences of anti-social behaviour and bullying, fewer children on report or being excluded, improved attendance, less stress and better home–school links with more parents becoming involved in the life of the school.

As Emotional Intelligence is seen as relevant to everyone, it is hoped that the effect will emanate outwards from the schools and into the community beyond, producing a happier and healthier population. If successful, the Education Department hopes to replicate the project throughout the city.

Discovery's EQ kitbag for happy healthy pupils

'Discovery is seeing the same thing everybody else sees and thinking something different.'

How should pupils be when they leave school, what needs to be in their kitbags?

❋ As many of the EQ attributes as possible. The vital one is self-awareness

❋ An acceptance of the importance of Life Long Learning

❋ Healthy self-esteem and self-belief

❋ Strong set of values

❋ Integrity

❋ Ability to accept others and work collaboratively

❋ Goals, dreams, ambitions

❋ Qualifications that demonstrate numeracy and literacy and the ability to understand, remember and assimilate knowledge and information

❋ High employability skills

❋ A desire to be happy and a knowledge of how to do that.

What state are children in when they arrive in school for the first time?

✳ Intuitive

✳ Open and willing

✳ Happy and sunny outlook

✳ Little sense of the concept of failure

✳ Already demonstrating key EQ attributes but unaware of them

✳ Curious.

Challenges:

✿ Don't know their individual learning styles or Multiple Intelligence strengths

✿ Some fearful and shut down

✿ Very limited vocabulary

✿ Some unable to work collaboratively

✿ Anti-social behaviour exhibited by some

✿ Some experiencing chaos, e.g. at home, and therefore in a chaotic state emotionally with little routine in their lives.

What must the learning environment have in place to ensure children make the journey through school acquiring the necessary contents for the EQ kitbag of life?

Offer every opportunity for every child and adult to grow and develop their EQ attributes and potential through:

✳ Collaboratively produced set of school values

✳ The actual physical environment

✳ EQ embedded in every moment of the school day

✳ The positive attitude and high expectations of adults

✳ Comprehensive training in and understanding of children's preferred learning styles, and intelligences

✳ Every lesson geared towards addressing the variety of learning styles and Multiple Intelligence

✳ Time spent daily on specifically nurturing EQ, e.g. meditation, affirmations, visualisation, Circle Time, Paths, and How To Be Happy, etc.

✳ High quality and regular CPD training offered to all staff

✳ Coaching, buddying, and mentoring all part of the school day

✳ Constant celebration and acknowledgement of positives

✳ Parents actively involved in helping out and taking part in training

✳ Philosophy of 'each one teach one' in place.

Cheryl Buggy, Project Director of 'Discovery'

69

So what?

If we accept the messages from Multiple Intelligences and from others such as David Perkins (Reflective Intelligence) and Daniel Goleman and others (Emotional Intelligence), how will this affect our classroom practice?

All teachers of Thinking for Learning are not expert in providing for all of these in detail but having recognised the truths in these theories, their classrooms tend to reflect the following:

1 Safe learning environment

2 Variety of task/activity

3 Choice of method/outcome

4 Collaboration and talk

5 Reflective questioning.

◆ Relationships, expectations and aspirations

> We can teach students what constitutes good thinking, but without their being motivated and disposed to engage in good thinking when the occasion arises, such instruction comes to naught.
>
> *John Dewey* [31]

This quote might connect with how you feel about some students – those who do not seem to *want* to learn. How do we persuade them that it is worthwhile developing and using their Thinking Skills? They need to know 'what's in it for me?' These are the pupils that Daniel Goleman would describe as needing to develop their Emotional Intelligence and the disposition for learning. Ann Brown talks about creating a climate in which pupils become 'Intentional Learners'. [32]

This is precisely what a number of researchers and practitioners have been working on. They have found ways to engage pupils and develop the intention to learn, inspiring them to come to school wanting to learn new skills and knowledge, and not just to please the teacher and get through the day. There are too many disruptive pupils in some schools; in others too many who are simply compliant and passive and without the drive to learn.

Thinking for Learning offers no panaceas in this respect but a number of developments offer great promise if implemented positively by schools and teachers. Below are a few examples, beginning with an outline of one that was mentioned earlier.

The BASICS model

For children to feel valued, they need BASICS. The following descriptions are based upon Alistair Smith's model.[7, 24] They are only a brief outline, but they make the point well. If pupils are to meet with **success**, teachers must provide them with an environment where they feel psychologically **safe** to attempt each **challenge** put before them. They need to feel that they **belong**, where the sense of the individual's **identity** leads to appropriate **aspirations**.

Belonging
Pupils who don't develop this sense of shared goals find it difficult to fit in and make friends. They may become bullies or victims. To include them:

♥ Encourage collaborative activities.

♥ Celebrate collective achievement.

♥ Use individual, paired and group activities.

♥ Foster interest in each others' interests and families.

Aspirations
Without self-motivation or the intention to learn pupils lack engagement.

★ Use analogies to help them see relevance.

★ Use Thinking Skills to engage them.

★ Teach and celebrate Multiple Intelligences.

★ Use positive role models from their own experience.

★ Find success and build upon it.

Safety
For some, school is a very stressful place – pupils too! Anxiety about being picked on by teachers or peers causes withdrawal or confrontation.

✚ Use fair and consistent application of rules.

✚ Avoid 'put-downs' and sarcasm.

✚ Take an interest in pupils as individuals.

✚ Use positive reinforcement.

✚ Develop the Community of Enquiry philosophy.

Identity

A lack of sense of self makes accepting criticism or praise difficult and inhibits risk taking.

! Use frequent and fair feedback.

! Explore personal histories and culture.

! Celebrate something special and unique about everyone.

! Provide opportunities to express emotion/feelings (Philosophy for Children/Drama/Circle Time).

! Establish conventions about the use of vocabulary between pupils.

Challenge

For learning to take place, pupils must be challenged in a safe and supportive manner.

❖ Provide differentiated tasks, which are achievable, but 'stretch' the learner.

❖ Challenge any limiting self-beliefs – they get in the way of learning!

❖ Discourage negative self-talk.

❖ Use timed tasks, particularly to challenge boys.

Success

Confident students take risks and expect success.

✓ Discourage comparisons with others.

✓ Celebrate individual success, targets met.

✓ Find time to celebrate success/expertise in hobbies, etc.

✓ Explain about negative self-talk.

✓ Practise positive self-talk and affirmations.

✓ Teach active listening skills for receiving feedback.

Robert Swartz: the National Center for Teaching Thinking, University of Massachusetts[33]

Robert Swartz has worked with teachers on the infusion of critical Thinking Skills in their lessons over a number of years. Whilst he has often come across the argument that some pupils need to develop their disposition towards learning before they can take advantage of Thinking Skills lessons, he disagrees. His observation is that the very Thinking Skills approach implicitly develops this disposition by engaging the learner very practically and by offering success to all.

Five basic components in these types of lessons seem to make them successful:

1 They are of practical help to students by providing **explicit strategies** to encourage success.

2 They build in **reflection time** for evaluating and celebrating our Thinking Skills (metacognition).

3 There is **practical engagement** in active thinking tasks that absorb the learner.

4 Pupils are taught how to transfer these skills and see their **relevance** in their daily lives.

5 They are conducted in an **open classroom environment** where good thinking attitudes are modelled and valued and pupils are safe to explore their thinking.

Whilst there are some students who are so negative that they cannot, or will not, get involved in such lessons, these are relatively few. For that much larger number who are often disaffected and disengaged, Thinking Skills offers them a way of becoming more engaged, more successful, and more disposed to learning. His argument, then, is that Thinking Skills, a component of Thinking for Learning, should in itself instigate our pupils becoming 'intentional learners', developing in them an appropriate disposition for learning.

Anne Kite: A Guide to Better Thinking[34]

Anne Kite has developed a programme for raising self-esteem and improving critical thinking in her Edinburgh Primary School. It follows an easy, six-step programme.

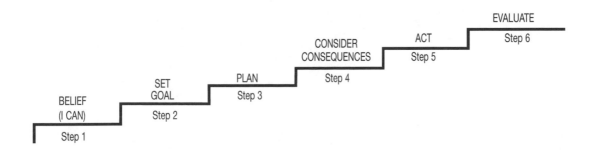

Thinking for Learning

A simple notion, but by taking pupils through a programme that illustrates how this works great gains have been seen in their self-esteem, their aspirations and, hence, their success.

Primed for learning

These are only three ideas that have been proved successful by classroom practitioners. There are doubtless others, or variations of these, which may achieve the same ends. What is important, though, is the premise with which we began this section: pupils need to be ready and motivated for learning before any can take place. If they are worried by school, distracted by external problems or fear failure, then even the most engaging lesson may fail that individual. As teachers we cannot deal with all of their problems, but we can create a supportive and safe haven within our classrooms in which they can arrive and look forward to learning.

Review

1. Devise five types of groupings you can use for small group work in your teaching.

2. Bloom's Taxonomy provides a hierarchy of thinking, but it is wrong to assume that the higher levels are inaccessible to 'less able' students. What variety of tasks could you set for your class that would challenge the whole ability range to demonstrate synthesis from earlier understanding in the same topic?

3. Multiple Intelligence theory suggests that every child has a unique set of intelligences and is special in some way. Using the class register, quickly note down something that every child has shown as a strength. Try not to limit your observations to traditional school values; it can be as unusual as 'incredible, unconscious dexterity twiddling his pen when thinking'. Next use the bibliography at the end of the book to learn how to maximise the potential of your pupils through using their Multiple Intelligences.

4. How might you utilise the suggestions on developing children's Emotional Intelligence to improve your pupils' EQ?

cont . . .

Thinking for learning activity: venn diagram

Venn diagrams are used for classification and to clarify relationships between factors. They require the participant to place statements either entirely within one category, or partially within two or three, as can be seen below.

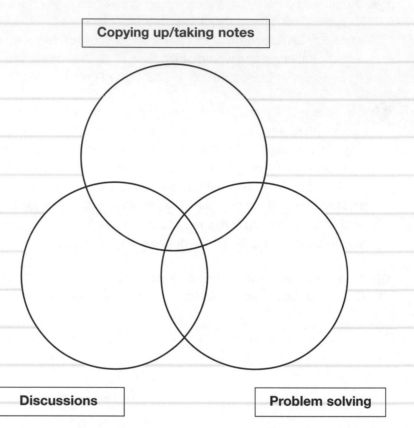

Copying up/taking notes

Discussions

Problem solving

Monitor your classroom activities for a week and place the activities in the relevant (parts of the) circles. Are you reverting to one particular type of activity? Carry out a straw poll with a class to identify how they would like to learn and compare it to the survey at the beginning of the chapter.

Chapter 3

Thinking teachers

Preview

Helping the pupils through effective mediation to make sense of what they are doing

What can be done to encourage thinking behaviours in the classroom

The importance of de-briefing

This chapter will provide explanations of what is important for **Thinking Teachers** to learn effectively, specifically:

Approaching talking about thinking: metacognition

Selecting an environment that is right for you

Assessing formatively: what, why and how

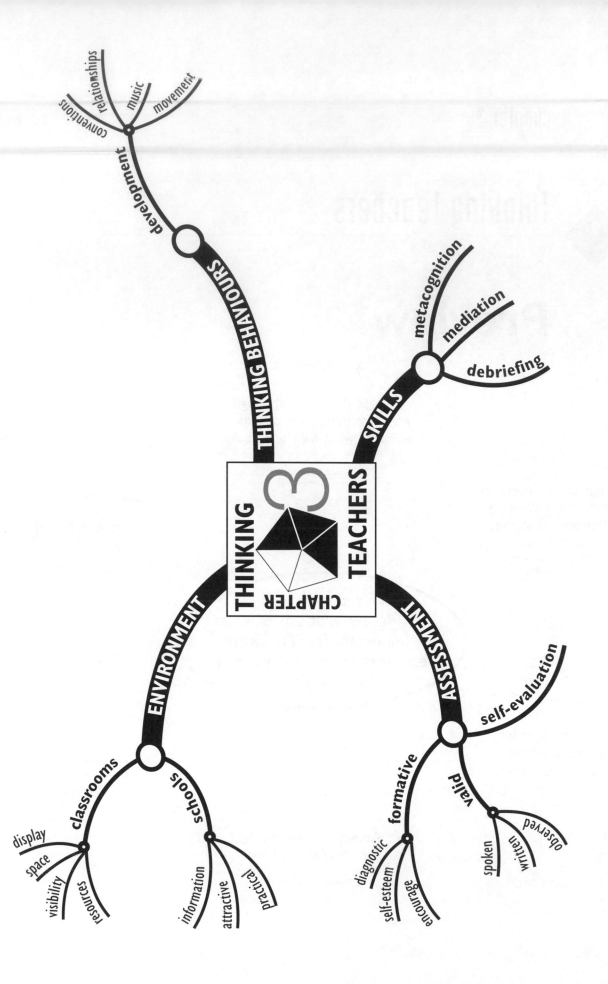

CHAPTER 3

THINKING TEACHERS

THINKING BEHAVIOURS
- development
  - conventions
  - relationships
  - music
  - movement

SKILLS
- metacognition
- mediation
- debriefing

ENVIRONMENT
- classrooms
  - display
  - space
  - visibility
  - resources
- schools
  - information
  - attractive
  - practical

ASSESSMENT
- self-evaluation
- formative
  - diagnostic
  - self-esteem
  - encourage
- valid
  - spoken
  - written
  - observed

◆ Encouraging thinking behaviours

Essentially this whole book is about 'thinking teachers'. Though we have constantly reiterated that it is the learner who is the focus of all our work, that it is the learner whom we would like to become skilful thinkers, it is the teacher who is the lead learner and who needs to put this work into practice. As you are reading this, you may already be to some extent a thinking teacher: you value the importance of the thought process, have identified a possible need for making the thinking processes more explicit in your classroom and wish to find out more. We think your reasoning is impeccable!

So we now turn our attention to the teacher in the classroom. Apart from putting these ideas into action, what else is it that the teacher might need to consider?

Relationships

There is a very human element to teaching in that it is partly about the dynamics of various relationships in the class. This is why classroom interactions are vital to learning. Sometimes new teachers or supply teachers may have difficulties with challenging groups of pupils mainly because there is no history of interaction there. It can take time for the teacher to become established.

Our goal is to aim for a true community of learners where the teacher is the lead learner and modelling what they wish to engender because within a Thinking for Learning environment everyone in the classroom is a learner. In the majority of lessons there will be whole class discussion and elements of working together as pairs or in groups. Positive relationships are essential for this to work. We need to encourage positive talk and self-talk with some clearly agreed conventions about how we communicate. A strongly affirmative culture with lots of praise, constructive critical feedback and no put-downs or sarcasm should be our aim.

Classroom conventions

As the teacher, you are in control of the classroom and need to model your expectations of pupils in their behaviour and work. The importance of these conventions needs to be openly discussed and agreed. They might include:

☆ being punctual to all lessons.

☆ always welcoming the pupils, by name if possible, at the beginnings of lessons.

☆ varying seating arrangements as appropriate to the task and encouraging all pupils to work with all others at some point. (The teacher needs to control this from day one so that it is an expectation, not a challenge or cause of anxiety to pupils.)

☆ beginning lessons with a connecting activity and a preview of the Big Picture. Do not leave pupils guessing as to what this lesson is about. Make sure they are engaged in some activity, however small or short, at the beginning of the lesson.

☆ running lessons to a timetable, keeping up the pace, changing activities regularly and timing them. Avoid too much tangential discussion, it might interest a few pupils and yourself but it usually loses the majority.

☆ encouraging a style of classroom talk that is positive and values everyone's contributions. Whilst seeming contrived at first it helps many pupils and overcomes outside influences. Encourage, through your example, pupils to refer to each other by name, to respond to each other's views and ideas and to prefix these responses with 'I agree/disagree with ... because ...'.

Movement

Get up and go: a new dictum from the National Literacy Strategy. We know that optimum conditions for learning include the opportunity for movement and physical breaks, especially ones with co-ordinated, cross-lateral movement to improve connections in the brain.[24] Use these breaks as an opportunity to review the work done so far and the processes used or to check whether any of the explicit lesson objectives have been reached.

So our classrooms need to allow a degree of movement for pupils. Teachers also need to be able to move around the room freely so as to keep attention and to intervene or eavesdrop when pupils are working individually or in pairs or groups. What we should always avoid as teachers is being rooted to that small space at the front of the class. The key message to the pupils then becomes that that is your legitimate space and any movement into their territory becomes a threat. If we allow it, we know that some pupils, often the more reluctant learners, will sit as far away from the teacher as possible and will choose not to participate. But it is the teacher who controls the classroom layout and conventions. Be flexible with room layout, change it as appropriate and make the whole room your territory.

Music

Our Thinking Classroom is a stimulating environment where a strong collaborative ethos exists. The learning here can be enhanced by the judicious use of music. The type of music to be used will depend on what the teacher is aiming to achieve. But beware of using contemporary popular music, as pupils can become distracted by this and the choice of what music to play becomes problematic – not a good stimulus for collaboration!

We have visited a number of classrooms where background music has been used to good effect. Examples of some of its uses include:

✴ To create a positive, up-beat atmosphere as pupils enter the classroom.

✴ To energise pupils when we want to encourage a faster pace, to get things done.

✴ To create a relaxed atmosphere of attentiveness.

✴ To delineate time on task.

For more detailed discussion on this topic see *the alps approach* by Alistair Smith and Nicola Call. [35]

◆ The teacher as mediator

One of the greatest causes of failure in school is the attempt by many teachers to remain neutral towards the material they are conferring on children. Instead of seeing themselves as mediators of values and morality they often seek to act as objective perpetrators of information, after some notion of an academic tradition.

Howard Sharron & Martha Coulter [10]

Sharron and Coulter are writing here about the work of Dr Reuven Feuerstein in Israel and his work on Instrumental Enrichment. Feuerstein developed the theory that the reason for the apparent 'backwardness' of many young learners in Israel during the 1950s and 1960s was due to an almost total lack of adult mediation in their learning experiences. Being deprived from a very young age of a caring adult to help them make meanings from the stimulus they were subjected to these young people became passive and lethargic. We occasionally come across these characteristics in our own classrooms. It is equally true that the lack of adult mediation of their behaviour can lead some children to behave badly. Having inappropriate or inadequate role models to fall back on and little ingrained valuing of the education system, such pupils may find school a difficult place.

Feuerstein's model of mediation between the stimulus and the learner (see page 21) can be seen closer to home in the work of the CASE (Cognitive Acceleration in Science Education) project.[1]

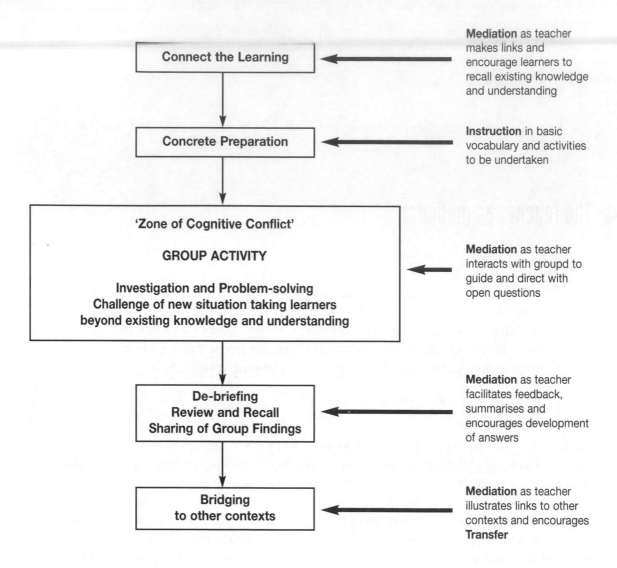

In the role of mediator the teacher is truly in a teaching situation. As the activity or discussion begins to uncover what the learner already knows and understands, and their existing preconceptions, the teacher can develop and extend this understanding through skilful prompting and questioning. When clear misconceptions and errors are obvious, the teacher mediates effectively by addressing and correcting these in a constructive and positive atmosphere of collaborative learning. Many teachers have found that even those pupils who can be difficult in the classroom are attracted by this style of learning and drawn into the learning community through their innate interest in the problem-solving process and the community dynamic.

Similar mediation is present in all Thinking Skills interventions. In these the teacher is seen as a resource for learning, sometimes providing information directly, sometimes as the head learner who leads and helps others to make sense of new situations and to think in a skilful and reasonable way.

Effective mediation involves:

➤ connecting the learning to previous experience.

➤ devising activities that are challenging but accessible (Vygotsky's 'Zone of Proximal Development').

➤ listening carefully to pupil talk.

➤ posing open questions to probe understanding.

➤ asking supplementary questions to develop meaning.

➤ summarising what they think a pupil has said (but not adding to/correcting at this point).

➤ inviting/encouraging interactions between pupils.

➤ providing factual answers when appropriate.

➤ allowing processing (thinking) time after posing questions.

➤ encouraging pupil talk in pairs/groups to clarify understanding.

◆ Metacognition

Because we're actually like … talking about it, we think, 'Oh yeah that's a new skill – I can use that in other lessons.' But if we hadn't been talking about it, I wouldn't have recognised it.

Year 9 history pupil

You're more likely to use new skills in different lessons because you've discussed it and given it a name … what you're doing. That gives you more chance to use it and know when to use it … it sort of has an impact on your memory and then you use it in other places.

Year 10 geography pupil

I knew what it all meant but I couldn't sort of describe it properly. Then I remembered the Concept Maps we'd used in geography. So I tried that and it really helped to me see it all and how it fits together.

Year 11 science pupil

These pupils are showing signs of metacognition. Younger pupils do this too (see pages 110–18). It is something we come across all too rarely in teaching: pupils who take enough interest in their own learning to want to talk about their learning skills – not the subject matter. We can encourage this by using a Thinking for Learning approach that might include some of the strategies suggested in this book or one of many others available.

How to encourage metacognition

* The best way to encourage pupils to think about thinking is to model the process yourself – show pupils that you are thinking about your own thinking and learning and that you are also interested in their thinking.

* Plan to use activities that challenge pupils to listen actively, to select, classify and justify choices and – most importantly – to *talk* about their thinking.

* Take time to de-brief pupils thoroughly at the end of such activities.

* A good example of such an activity is included in *Thinking Through Geography* [14] in the section 'Story-Telling' (see page 139).

Teachers involved in Thinking Skills have become increasingly convinced that it is when pupils begin to get involved in conversations about how they learn (metacognition) that learning really begins and their dispositions towards learning improve. Even simply questioning how they arrived at a particular answer, discussing it with a classmate or using the language of thinking when referring to the process they have used are forms of metacognition.

Effective thinkers reflect on their learning and the process by which they reached a particular outcome. As we plan to provide our pupils with processing time, so these learners have become trained in not impulsively articulating answers. Instead their responses are always considered. To reach this stage they need to have been provided with a secure framework by the teacher that encourages them to think about their thinking. Slowly, the teacher's explicit structure will be removed, leaving the learner to explore instinctively their own thinking.

◆ De-briefing

As in the National Literacy Strategy's use of the plenary, pupils' understanding needs to be uncovered during and on completion of tasks. De-briefing aims to do this. Teachers who use Thinking for Learning frequently debrief pupils after the activities in order to develop each one's metacognitive abilities. The debriefing session encourages them to reflect upon and talk about how they worked towards a solution, and how they might use and improve upon such strategies in the future. Debriefing can be difficult at first, especially with pupils who are not used to this sort of approach and who may lack the vocabulary necessary for thinking and talking about these processes. The language of metacognition needs to be developed. However, when they are used to it most pupils find de-briefing beneficial because it:

* helps them to review and consolidate the new learning that has taken place.

* encourages them all to participate, to listen actively and to learn from their peers.

* makes new learning skills explicit; for example, ways of classifying or prioritising.

* illustrates the value of collaboration and co-operation.

* enables them to see links between things.

* develops their literacy skills because they have to articulate and structure their reasons.

* helps them to see how and where they can use their new Thinking Skills in other contexts (transfer).

* by making the thinking process explicit or visible (metacognition), it helps them to understand how they learn best.

* values difference in the way that pupils think and learn and so celebrates individual strengths rather than identifying deficiencies.

Go to page 140 for a practical example of de-briefing

◆ Assessment in the thinking classroom

Studies show that innovations which include strengthening the practice of formative assessment produce significant, and often substantial, learning gains.

Paul Black & Dylan Wiliams [36]

The work of Paul Black and Dylan Wiliams is now well known in teaching circles and the underlying principles of formative assessment are clearly seen in Thinking for Learning lessons. Summative assessment has indicated the results that can be achieved. CASE and Thinking Through Geography have raised GCSE grades by between 0.5 and 1 full grade on average. It is how formative assessment helps achieve this that is significant.

What is formative assessment?

Unlike summative assessment, which summarises a pupil's apparent ability at a specific point in time, formative assessment helps the teacher to identify the needs of the pupil through assessing what learning has occurred up to that point. The information is used to help the learner rather than to provide a judgement.

The assessment itself also needs to be appropriate for the purpose. Valid assessments should provide pupils with the opportunity to show what they have learnt about what the teacher wants the assessment to measure. Sometimes the assessment activity can get in the way of measuring the learning that is to be assessed. For example, a written test to measure understanding of a topic might not be the best medium for somebody who best expresses themselves orally. Naturally, the weakness in the written work needs addressing, but that is for a future lesson and a future assessment to measure progress. Here, the learner is being tested for comprehension. The importance of teachers' understanding of their pupils is again an important factor.

Another side to the validity of assessment activities is whether they are simply measuring recall or not. Sometimes this may be what is required. But primarily we want to encourage thinking pupils, so higher level skills, such as analysis need to be tested. The alternative is that lessons become a series of 'improve your memory' classes, with only techniques for memorising taught alongside the subject.

So in Thinking for Learning we need to think about assessing the processes that are taking place. At a basic level this has been happening for years in maths, as pupils are asked to 'show their working'. Thinking pupils need to 'show their thinking' if we are to monitor the progress of their cognitive processing. Quite often, as previously discussed, this takes place through dialogue, a valid medium for formative assessment that allows the teacher to provide immediate and educative feedback. That is, the teacher can praise the learning that has taken place and suggest where improvements might be made. This can be accomplished by the teacher listening in on discussion groups or through direct, one-to-one talk with the pupil. Wherever possible the dialogue should be both reflective and reflexive, so that the pupil can learn from the experience and formative assessment can truly be said to have taken place. For reasons of self-esteem, at no time should one pupil be compared to another.

However, formative assessment goes beyond the giving of educative feedback and praising pupils. Whatever evidence is gained through discussion, observation or written work can be used to adapt the teaching and learning activities that take place in the classroom so as to develop the pupils' learning. It is what happens within our classrooms that makes a difference to pupil achievement, what information on the learner's progress teachers can glean, not government initiatives, though these may influence classroom practice.

When formative assessment is used all pupils gain, but the lowest achievers gain most. This is true in all subjects, all age groups and all countries where studies have taken place.[36] Reflective discussion about activities, tests and success criteria can always be shown to improve performance. As an example take this piece of research into science education for a mixed ability group of 12-year-olds. A control group was taught and tested whilst the experimental group received the same teaching and test plus an emphasis on formative assessment in the process of the unit of work.

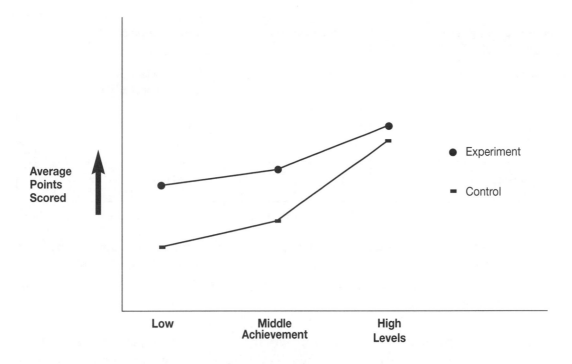

All pupils performed better with formative assessment. The lowest achievers gained most. The middle achievers in the experimental group performed as well as the high achievers in the control group.

What is wrong with most classroom assessment?

➡ It tends to be superficial and often does not go beyond bland praise.

➡ It does not include pupils in the assessment process; they simply receive feedback.

➡ It over emphasises quantity and presentation at the expense of quality and understanding.

➡ There is too much attention paid to marks and grades and not enough to learning.

➡ It encourages competition and norm-referencing and demotivates all but the highest attainers.

Marking and grading

One of the most entrenched practices in teaching is the insistence on marking all pieces of work and on awarding marks, grades, and now even levels to pupils' work. And yet all the research shows that this does not work. Black and Wiliams summarise it as follows:

Groups of pupils given:	Improvement in work	Interest in subject
A Marks only (inc. grades)	Nil	+ For high attainers - For middle/low attainers
B Marks (grades) + comments	Nil	+ For high - For middle/low
C Comments only	30%	+ For all groups

Giving only marks or grades has no impact on the standard of pupils' work and demotivates most of them by establishing a negative set of beliefs about their ability in this subject. Adding comments to help pupils improve their work has no effect either! They are still unduly influenced by the mark.

Writing only comments on the work improves the standard by 30 per cent, especially if pupils are then expected to respond to these. Additionally, all groups of pupils throughout the attainment range respond positively when there is no grade. Due to learners also being affected by the ingrained exercise of grading, there may initially be some protest, but they will soon adapt and benefit from this practice. To make the marking even more useful to them as learners, if the comments are added at the drafting stage of an assignment then the final piece of work can be influenced by them and the teacher's comments will immediately have had an effect on their learning.

The main beneficiary of assessment must be the individual child, and therefore the main purposes must be diagnosis and motivation.

Gipps and Stobart[37]

The motivation, we believe, comes as the learners begin to see the progress that they are making. Remember that we have already helped them to adopt a positive attitude to learning through methods outlined in the previous chapter, including the thinking strategies used in the Thinking for Learning classroom. Once pupils move into this successful cycle, the motion becomes self-perpetuating and self-esteem and success begin to grow together.

But adding useful, constructive comments to pupils' work is time consuming! So what do we do?

* Stop thinking that everything a pupil does has to be marked – and educate pupils and parents to understand that most work is preparation and that final outcomes depend upon it being done (not marked).

* Focus 'marking' time on selected pieces of work that are most likely to improve pupil performance.

* Find time to discuss your comments with pupils, especially those in most need on particular pieces of work.

What else can we do to encourage formative assessment?

> The best way to encourage effective involvement is to expect it from an early age and make it part of normal learning activity, using techniques appropriate to particular needs and circumstances, rather than bolting it on as something separate.
>
> *Sutton* [38]

One method of 'effective involvement' is teaching the pupils to self-evaluate. If they could be shown how to be constructively critical about their own work, we are part of the way to creating independent learners. First, the reason for learning a particular skill or topic should be made clear to them, so that they know what it is that they have to achieve. If the criteria on which they are to be assessed are transparent, then they will have something tangible to aim for. Second, encouraging self-analysis (such as in a learning log) of what they found challenging or how they went about resolving a certain issue will make them think about the process that they went through. This can sometimes be a useful tool in helping them to evaluate strengths and where improvements might be made.

According to Black and Wiliams the following would also be useful – they are all characteristics of Thinking for Learning lessons:

* Make activities challenging and interesting.

* Use short, closed questions for review and recall but not for assessment.

* Use more 'open' questions that require pupils to think.

* Allow more Processing Time before expecting pupils to answer. If they can answer straight away, they did not have to think!

* Encourage pupils to develop their answers, and to speak beyond the usual 1 or 2 seconds normally seen.

* Encourage paired discussion in response to questions.

* Move away from the 'hands-up' approach that excludes too many pupils. After a period of processing time in pairs expect all pairs to have an answer.

* Expect other pupils to evaluate and respond to the answers given by their peers.

* Use ambiguous, open activities to encourage exploration of ideas.

✳ Encourage pupils to 'set' questions from what they have learned rather than answering your questions. They can ask one another questions they have devised. This helps you to evaluate what they have understood and then to reform their questions (and understanding) when their peers do not understand the question.

✳ Use tests for review purposes only, as a diagnosis for pupils of what they need to concentrate on, not as a summary of their 'ability'.

Assessment is multi-faceted, but we must not lose sight of its purpose. It is there to help the teacher to help the students get the most from their learning; it should not be used as a tool with which to brand pupils as 'successes' or 'failures', nor to indicate which schools are 'making the grade'.

◆ The learning environment

The context of the classroom

Many of our schools have made huge strides in recent years in extending the learning environment beyond the restrictions of the individual classroom. A lot of attention has been paid to the whole school environment, the physical environment and the development of libraries into learning resource centres. However, in most of our schools the traditional classroom remains the focus for most of the planned teaching and learning activity during the day. Of course much of the real learning takes place everywhere but in the classroom – in the corridors, in the playground, on the way to and from school. It is essential that the classroom is not an isolated island but just one component in a whole learning environment.

In the best schools we are privileged to visit there is a feeling of a learning community that starts even at the school gates – at one school these had been purpose designed by an artist in residence together with the pupils! The outdoor area of this particular school contains a hard play area with games and artwork painted on the ground and walls; there are interesting and attractive sitting areas as well as spaces for ball games and wildlife, and cultivated areas cared for by groups of pupils. The school entrance is welcoming and informative and there is always someone there to greet the visitor – often pupils take on this role in rotation. Foyers and corridors contain examples of pupils' art and other work. The area where a particular year group or department is found has an identity of its own. As we walked into the Year 5 or the science department we knew it – the walls and signs told us so and they displayed a sense of pride in these places. I am interested; I want to learn too!

The above is no fabled Utopia. Such schools exist. If you are lucky, you teach in one. Unfortunately different scenarios can also be found. Sometimes a very attractive and purposeful classroom has been created but exists within a desert of dirty and uncared-for corridors in a school where the visitor has difficulty locating the entrance and the school grounds are litter strewn and neglected. Both extremes can be found in all types and styles of schools. We know of two schools in the same town in northern England, built in the 1920s with no school fields of their own. One is a rather shabby, down-at-heel building that depressed us as soon as we walked through the door. The other is approached through a playground that has been transformed into a delightful learning, playing and relaxing area with the addition of raised flower beds, seating areas and artwork. The entrance to the school is clean, feels modern and always has an up-to-date display of pupils' work. The classrooms are vibrant, exciting places to be. Both schools receive the same funding.

Characteristics of a thinking classroom

In her 1999 report for the DfEE, 'From Thinking Skills to Thinking Classrooms',[8] Carol McGuinness recognised a shift in emphasis within the move towards a more informed teaching methodology. She perceived a development from the view of thinking as a set of skills towards a more holistic thinking curriculum, thinking classroom or thinking school.

The Thinking Classroom is influenced by a set of factors that include:

- curriculum design
- curricular materials/resources
- teachers' pedagogy
- teacher beliefs about learning
- continuing professional developments for teachers.

Where a number of these factors coincide we can find classrooms where a particular style of learning is taking place, one mentioned on pages 47–8 by Ann Brown and her research colleagues is a Community of Learners.

In this classroom teachers have found or developed the resources to suit their preferred style of teaching. They have taken ownership of the curriculum, shaping and planning it so that it meets the needs of both the learner and the prescriptions of the National Curriculum. They see themselves as lead learners in the classroom with their own on-going professional development needs being met partly by research in their own classrooms, and supported by networks within the school or the wider educational community.

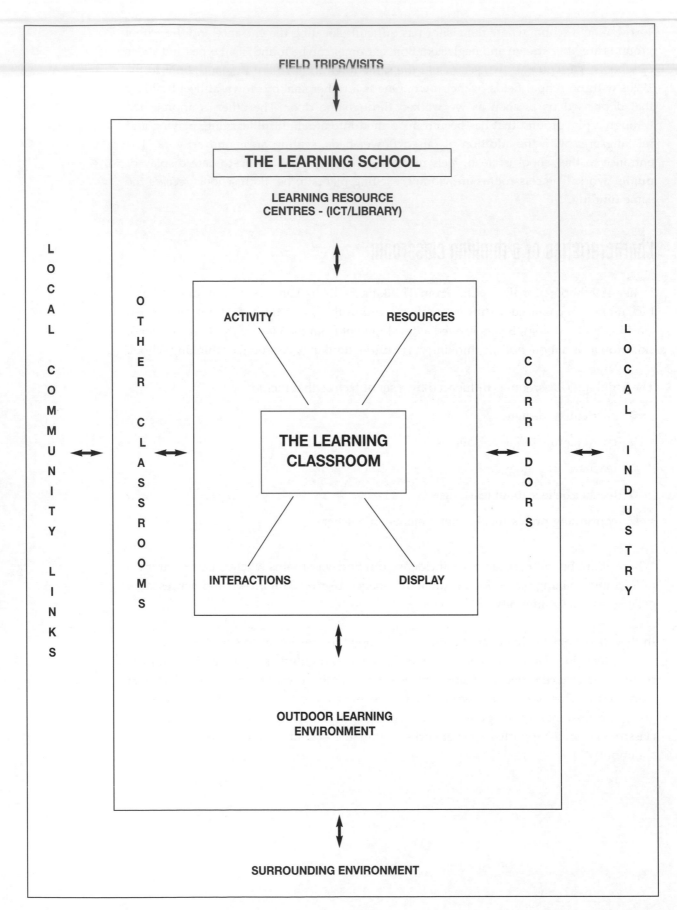

FIELD TRIPS/VISITS

THE LEARNING SCHOOL

LEARNING RESOURCE
CENTRES - (ICT/LIBRARY)

LOCAL COMMUNITY LINKS

OTHER CLASSROOMS

ACTIVITY

RESOURCES

THE LEARNING
CLASSROOM

INTERACTIONS

DISPLAY

CORRIDORS

LOCAL INDUSTRY

OUTDOOR LEARNING
ENVIRONMENT

SURROUNDING ENVIRONMENT

The Learning Environment

The physical environment

In the Thinking Classroom certain types of activity and relationships are likely to occur and the layout of the room needs to reflect and allow this. Cluttered, overcrowded rooms with fixed rows of desks are not going to make this easy. Some key features to strive for are:

1 Flexibility

Sometimes we want to work as a whole class, sometimes individually, in pairs or groups. Be flexible with the layout of furniture and develop certain styles of arrangement that pupils will come to associate with types of learning. Pin a laminated plan of these different arrangements on the wall.

2 Space

It is important to have one area in the room clear of furniture and clutter, where pupils can move freely, make presentations, etc. This will help the smooth running of lessons and help with classroom management issues.

3 Ease of movement

As pupils may be moving between groups, accessing resources, etc. they need to be able to move around reasonably freely.

4 Resources

Research shows that learning is stimulated and accelerated when a wide variety of learning resources are deployed together. Resources need to be kept where pupils can have easy access to them when needed. The physical resources, such as paper, pencils, ICT facilities should be stored around the room in locations where access is straightforward and movement to get them causes the least disturbance. In some classrooms the actual learning resources – books, worksheets, photographs, etc. – are laid out in a central position. Differentiated materials can be clearly colour-coded or labelled to allow pupils to take responsibility for selecting their own level of work when this is thought appropriate. On the whole, however, there is far too much emphasis on creating learning materials at different levels that will be used by particular groups of pupils. This can have a profoundly demoralising effect, lowering motivation, aspiration and self-esteem if not handled well. In most cases the styles of learning advocated by Thinking for Learning preclude the need for many differentiated materials.

A recommended resource for those who doubt that even relatively weak learners can succeed with difficult text and visual materials are the series of packs for developing literacy produced by Nicholas Roberts.[39]

Visibility

One of the keys to success with Thinking for Learning is the quality of interactions between teacher and pupils, and between pupils. For this to happen it is important to ensure that the teacher can always maintain eye contact with pupils and circulate easily around the room. Equally, pupils need to be able to see one another and not constantly be listening to pupils who are behind them – as will inevitably happen when desks are in regimented rows.

6 Clutter free/noise friendly

Some classrooms seem to over fill with bags and coats so that moving around becomes a health and safety risk! Establish conventions for the neat and tidy storage of these items from the start. Explain to pupils why it is important.

Equally, thinking activities involve a lot of talk and generally generate a degree of noise – strange when you think about it! Classrooms designed to dampen this down are best – carpets on the floor, fabrics on windows and/or in corners all help.

Thinking classrooms and display areas

Used thoughtfully and constructively the walls of our classrooms can be a useful resource for learning and thinking. In the primary school, in first and middle schools, this is already apparent to some degree as pupils' work is displayed, providing a retrospective celebration of what they have achieved. This is good as far as it goes and we would recommend that one area is always devoted to this use. However, the emphasis is too often on appearances, with the work to some extent being used as 'wallpaper'.

In many secondary classrooms we also see positive use of wall space but sometimes this is not the case and what could be a learning resource is at best sterile space and, at worst, an eyesore.

Wall space can be used for a number of useful purposes including:

LEARNING WALL:		CELEBRATION WALL:	
Learning questions*	On-going enquiry	Record of pupil work	
Key vocabulary*	Brainstorm	Artwork and 3-D (changed regularly)	
PUPIL WALL:		INFORMATION WALL:	
Pupil interests	Topical	Posters	Information display
Personal histories		Maps	Photographs

*   *Note: Research shows that Key Vocabulary and Questions will become embedded in the learner's mind if they are displayed prominently above eye level and used as part of learning activities.*

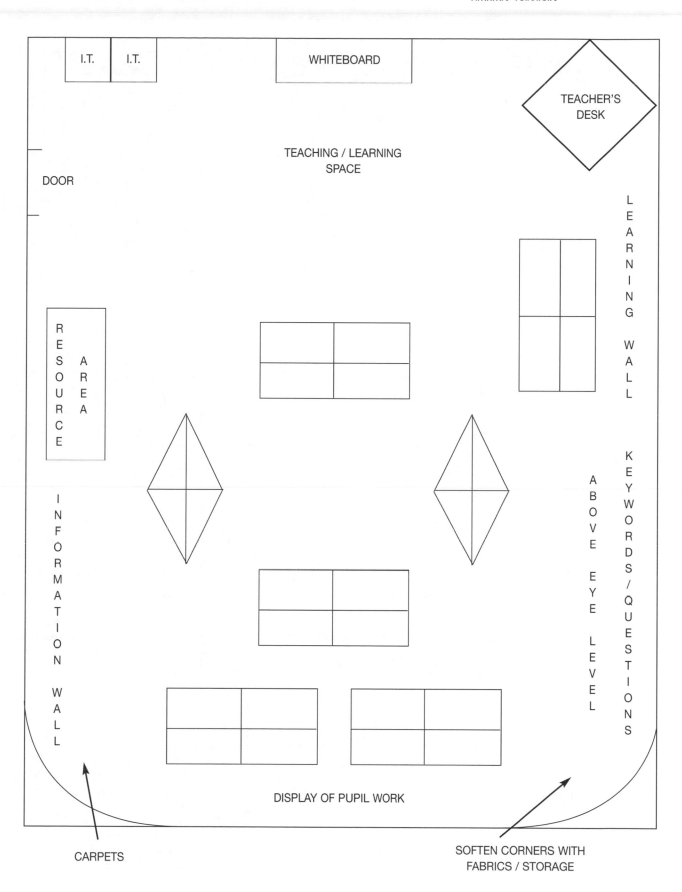

A Thinking Classroom (1)

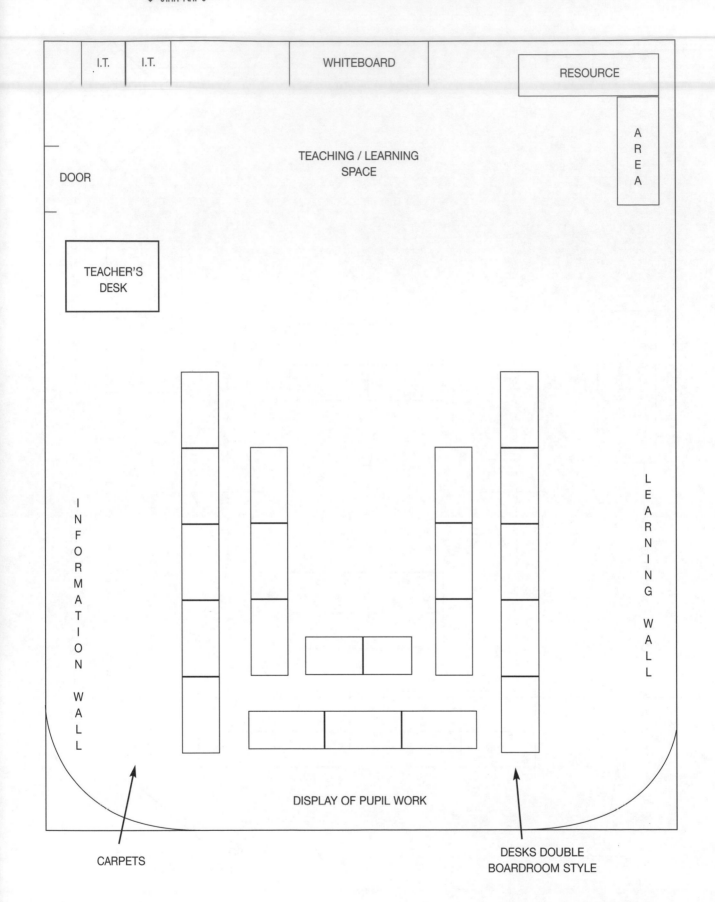

A Thinking Classroom (2)

Ryles Park

At Ryles Park High School in Macclesfield we saw excellent examples of the constructive use of wall space in the humanities department. Particularly effective were the learning and information displays.

◎ A large rainforest 'tree' adorned one corner, adding colour, interest and keywords to that area of the classroom.

◎ Keywords also surrounded displays relating to the various ongoing topics. Pictures/posters were used to provide the focal point, whilst keywords surrounded them. All were above the pupils' eye level and are referred to during lessons.

◎ Definitions of key vocabulary were displayed as above.

◎ A display about Italy, which included a map, money, food packets and labels, provided an informative and attractive backdrop to work done on the country.

◎ Reminders, such as 'Keep to the Point of the Question', pepper the walls to be referred to during preparation for writing.

◎ Other tips for writing are visible to the pupils for use whilst they are writing. These include reminders such as (under a heading 'Retelling') 'Use the past tense'.

Choosing a learning environment for your classroom

The ways in which teachers and schools choose to organise their classrooms and the learning experiences they provide for pupils depends largely upon what they believe about education, its purpose and the nature of intelligence. Of course, values and attitudes affect our lives in myriad ways. They also have a great influence on how our pupils view the learning experiences we provide.

The statements below are designed to reveal how you view learning, and this in turn will affect how comfortable you feel in different types of classroom setting. It sometimes comes as a surprise to some of our colleagues when they discover that we do not share a common set of values and understandings about learning even though we may have assumed that we do. Before setting out on any fundamental change to the way we teach, or even to how we arrange our classroom, it is well worth spending some time exploring and discussing such issues. In this way a common understanding about effective teaching and learning can be established in the school, department or year group.

'Fact or Opinion' exercises are commonly used in Thinking for Learning and in Literacy lessons. This is a relatively simple technique that can be used in a number of ways. For example:

* Pupils highlight a piece of text to identify facts and opinions, in two different colours.

* Statements are presented on a diagram and pupils decide which are facts and which opinions.

* Statements are given out on cards and pupils divide them into 'Facts' or 'Opinions' (and probably 'Don't know').

Try sorting out these statements about education into 'Facts' and 'Opinions' with a group of colleagues.

1. Girls tend to achieve better results than boys in English schools.

2. Boys do better than girls in secondary education because they see a future in work.

3. Some types of intelligence are valued more highly than others in our education system.

4. The quality of leadership provided by the headteacher has a major effect on the educational standards in a school.

5. Comprehensive schools became the norm in England and Wales during the 1970s.

6. Intelligence is modifiable. Proven intervention strategies and skilful teachers can enhance pupils' levels of intelligence.

7. Teaching is easier with smaller groups of pupils.

8. Intelligence is measured by the use of IQ tests.

9. Children cannot think in the abstract until the age of 10–12.

10. Experiential and resource-based learning are the keys to successful teaching.

11. GCSE pass rates have been steadily improving throughout the 1990s.

12. The government set challenging targets for schools in relation to Literacy and Numeracy.

If you spend any time on this exercise with your peers or colleagues, you may well find that you do not agree on which statements are facts and which opinions. You may even come to the conclusion that it is not actually that straightforward. Some of the statements are affected by their historical context of course. Statement 2 was actually made in the late 1960s at a time when boys did achieve better results than girls at GCE. And of course we may need to discuss what 'doing better' really means.

Review

1 Note down your own list of classroom conventions to which you will be able to adhere over the next half term. Reflect on their success at the end of that period.

2 Experiment with music in your lessons. Put together a 'play list' that will help to demarcate time on task, create an up-beat atmosphere, energise pupils and create a relaxed atmosphere. After a week, ask the pupils what they enjoyed and whether they thought it helped them learn.

3 What questions might help pupils to think about their thinking/encourage metacognition?

4 In light of the research by Black and Wiliams, what specific strategies will you now employ to assess the work of your pupils?

Thinking for learning activity: diamond ranking

Diamond ranking is used to encourage discussion about the relative importance of certain factors. It demands that participants rank those factors, stating their single most important and least important considerations. However, it allows for more circumspection in the middle order, as can be seen below.

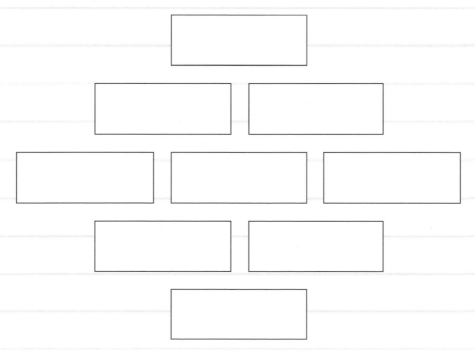

Identify nine ways to transform your classroom physically into a Thinking for Learning environment. Now prioritise these using the strategy above.

Chapter 4

Thinking schools

Preview

What characteristics the lessons should have, with an example from the Accelerated Learning component

Whether they work better in mixed ability settings or not

How an infusion lesson is structured, with an example from CASE

This chapter will provide explanations of how to develop **Thinking for Learning** strategies, specifically

Looking at a variety of Thinking for Learning strategies, together with rationale and practical examples wherever possible

How to establish a community of enquiry and run it successfully

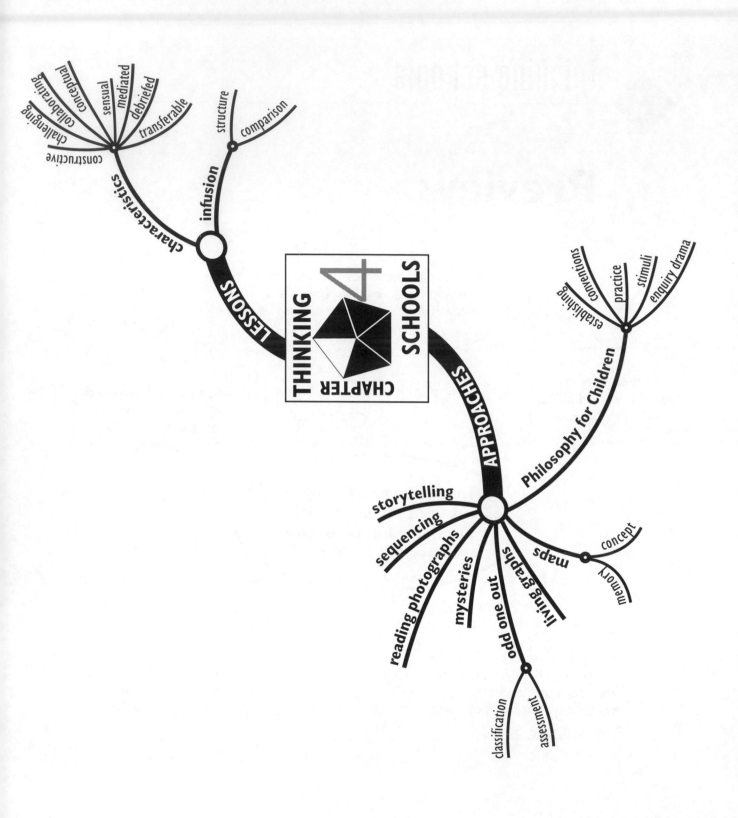

CHAPTER

4

THINKING SCHOOLS

LESSONS

characteristics

infusion

structure

comparison

constructive
challenging
collaborating
conceptual
sensual
mediated
debriefed
transferable

APPROACHES

Philosophy for Children

establishing
conventions
practice
stimuli
enquiry drama

storytelling

sequencing

reading photographs

mysteries

odd one out

living graphs

maps

concept

memory

classification

assessment

◆ Introducing thinking for learning to the classroom

The focus of this chapter will be the introduction of the Thinking for Learning strategies, including some practicalities for consideration: how several of the approaches work and how some of the important aspects of these approaches can be encouraged. We will be drawing upon the experiences of practitioners nationwide and hopefully stimulating ideas for practice in your own school. Most of the examples we provide can be adapted to any age group, subject or ability level. And it is with a brief section on ability that we begin.

Setting, streaming or mixed ability?

Thinking for Learning lessons have been taught successfully in all the approaches mentioned, but with differing levels of impact. 'Low' sets tend to be motivated by these lessons but often find some of the activities too challenging because they miss the potential interaction and thinking of higher achievers. Very high attaining sets sometimes find these lessons equally challenging as they take them out of their normal 'comfort zone' where they are used to success. This seems to be especially true of higher attaining girls, who often quietly conform to the lesson without feeling the need to push themselves any further.

It is interesting that beliefs about setting and streaming seem to be as entrenched and intransigent amongst educators as those about marking – probably even more so. And yet none of the available research supports what many teachers believe about the efficacy of setting.

The two most recent research papers on this subject, from the NFER and the Scottish office, are in general agreement about this topic, one of which is summarised below.

In the NFER Report, Sukhanandan and Lee[40] state:

* There is no evidence that homogeneous grouping, compared with mixed-ability grouping, produces beneficial outcomes for pupils.

* It is widely accepted homogeneous groupings have a negative impact on the achievement and school experiences of pupils of low ability and those of working class or ethnic minority backgrounds. Boys and summer-born children also do worse in homogeneous groups.

* Different forms of ability grouping are appropriate in different circumstances, so teachers and schools need to be flexible.

* Within class, ability groupings offer the best chance of success.

* Pupils needs could be met on a more individual basis through an increased emphasis on independent learning and improved library and ICT resources.

◆ Developing thinking for learning: characteristics

Successful Thinking for Learning strategies have all or most of the following characteristics in place.

Constructive

They take account of what pupils already know or believe about a topic. Prior learning is acknowledged and built upon. Pupils are involved or engaged in lessons from the start. In Alistair Smith's Accelerated Learning Cycle, this is known as 'Connecting the Learning'. The CASE lesson also recognises its importance through establishing the existing knowledge of pupils.

Challenging

Using activities that force pupils to think and to talk because the answers or solutions are not obvious. Whilst the tasks are challenging, and initially might seem too difficult, they are achievable. The ambiguity of many of the tasks means that there can be several 'right' answers and a sense of achievement for everyone. In CASE lessons, this is referred to as a period of Cognitive Conflict, and for Vygotskians, this is the Zone of Proximal Development.

Collaborative

Talk is essential to learning for many of us. By having to articulate our thoughts, we clarify them. Talking with others confirms/challenges our own understanding and adds to that of our peers. Learning to work together towards solutions develops our interpersonal skills and our understanding.

Conceptual

Achievement often becomes more difficult when we have to deal in big ideas or concepts. Most subjects have a limited number of big concepts that need to be understood. Thinking for Learning activities help to develop an understanding of these big concepts.

Sensual

Good Thinking for Learning strategies utilise a range of senses and pay attention to the preferred learning styles of individuals. A group of pupils normally divides roughly into three categories: visual, auditory and kinesthetic learners. According to Neuro-Linguistic Programming (NLP) most of us have a preference for one of these learning styles, although we do tend to use the other two as well. From their work it has been concluded that teacher input should be through a variety of these modalities.

Mediated and debriefed

Both the teacher and a student's peers play a key role in mediating the learning experience through active listening, asking appropriate questions, summarising and reviewing. De-briefing, both during and at the end of learning sessions, draws attention to what has been learned and how it has been learned.

Transfer

Skills and understandings developed by Thinking for Learning activities may be used in new contexts in other subjects within the curriculum and in real-life situations outside school. Transfer can be seen as the key aim of Thinking for Learning interventions – to equip young people with learning skills and dispositions that will serve them well in many different learning and living situations.

Accelerated learning as part of thinking for learning

The planning sheets on pages 106 and 107 were devised by Rachel Lofthouse (then at Prudhoe High School, now at the University of Newcastle) to incorporate the principles of Accelerated Learning into the planning of humanities lessons.

The way she has integrated her planning into Alistair Smith's Accelerated Learning Cycle shows the practicality of this particular approach. However, what is of interest to us is how what we have described above can be seen within the various stages of the cycle. All the components mentioned in the 'Characteristics' section are either implicit within the cycle (such as 'constructive'/connecting the learning, and challenge) or can be added (de-briefing, transfer, etc.) within this structure to develop a practical resource for planning. The strategies pioneered under the banner of 'Thinking Skills' can easily be incorporated at relevant points throughout the cycle.

◆ The structure of an infusion lesson

In Chapter 1 we discussed whether to infuse Thinking Skills into lessons or whether a 'bolt-on' generic course was better. Although both have their advantages (and for an example of a good bolt-on course we recommend Top Ten Thinking Tactics[20]), we argued that an infused approach provides a more holistic and sustained method for Thinking for Learning in the school. On page 108 we have provided the structure through which the infusion lessons can be delivered. The fact that, with infusion, opportunities across the curriculum should be sought to use Thinking Skills alongside subject content means that the Accelerated Learning Cycle lends itself to this approach as well. If lessons are planned using the cycle (above), then Thinking Skills strategies may be planned in, as much of the ethos of both approaches amalgamates under Thinking for Learning.

Within the structure outlined on page 108, we have identified the previously mentioned main characteristics of a Thinking for Learning lesson to exemplify at which stage each fits into its organisation. There are no inconsistencies in application between this structure and the Accelerated Learning Cycle.

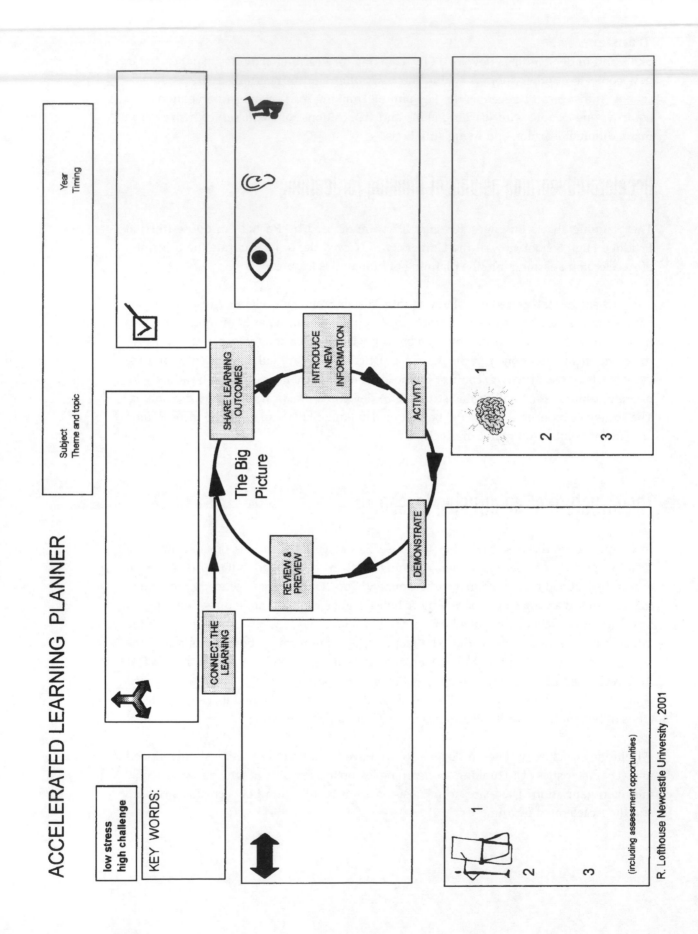

ACCELERATED LEARNING PLANNER

low stress
high challenge

KEY WORDS:

Subject
Theme and topic

Year
Timing

The Big
Picture

SHARE LEARNING
OUTCOMES

INTRODUCE
NEW
INFORMATION

ACTIVITY

DEMONSTRATE

REVIEW &
PREVIEW

CONNECT THE
LEARNING

1

2

3

1

2

3

(including assessment opportunities)

R. Lofthouse Newcastle University, 2001

ACCELERATED LEARNING PLANNER

Subject	Geography
Theme and topic	Climate – Andes
Year	9
Timing	1 hr 10 mins

low stress
high challenge

KEY WORDS:
ALTITUDE
RELIEF RAINFALL
CLIMATE

1 Understand why mountains experience a different weather to lowlands.
2 Learn about processes or relief rainfall.
3 Data-crunching practice.

Read extracts from 'Touching the Void'.

Afterwards brainstorm details about high mountain weather.

SHARE LEARNING OUTCOMES

1 Climate graph sheet – included Andes cool/wet (drier than TRF).
2 Temp decreases away from equator.
3 Convection rain caused by air rising.

INTRODUCE NEW INFORMATION

The Big Picture

Location determines the climate of an area.

Altitude affects climate.

ACTIVITY

1 Complete individual summary table of South American climate. Need data sheets and atlases.

2 Complete reasoning exercise 'Explaining South American Climates'.

3 AS CLASS look at relief rainfall sheet and discuss.
IN PAIRS complete true/false sheets (one each).

DEMONSTRATE

REVIEW & PREVIEW

CONNECT THE LEARNING

Climate of an area depends on 1) latitude, 2) altitude.

Rainfall always occurs due to air rising – but may rise for different reasons.

Next lesson – draw all weather work together.

NB go though tasks in class for pupil to self-assess.

1 Summary table)

2 Explanations

3 True/False ex

(including assessment opportunities)

R. Lofthouse Newcastle University, 2001

---

1 INTRODUCTION

Teacher introduces lesson by activating pupils' existing knowledge and establishing its relevance to the learning about to take place. Students' prior experience of the thinking process to be used is explored and the skill outcomes of the lesson are described.

↓

2 ACTIVE THINKING

The main learning activities of the lesson integrate the Thinking for Learning process with the subject content, using a range of strategies/graphic organisers as appropriate, that are collaborative, challenging and, where possible, deal with big ideas. New input should be delivered via visual, auditory and kinesthetic mediums and mediated by the teacher in order to include all learners.

↓

3 THINKING ABOUT THINKING

Students are prompted to think about how they have worked, what sort of thinking was involved and how effective it was. De-briefing is one of the strategies used here.

↓

4 APPLYING THINKING

Students are shown/consider how these Thinking Skills can be used in other situations, both in the same subject/lesson and in other subjects (near transfer), and beyond school (far transfer).

The structure of an infusion lesson

Features of CASE – how it relates to the infusion model

From the general characteristics, through Accelerated Learning and the structure of an infusion lesson, to this example, we have attempted to identify how the parts make up the whole in the Thinking for Learning lesson. It is important to remember at this stage that we are not solely advocating CASE lessons, but that this is one of many types of lesson that incorporates the characteristics we have discussed above. Others would include ACTS and Philosophy for Children, which would utilise such features of Thinking for Learning to a greater or lesser degree. Also of importance to remember is that these lessons are presented within the context of a safe learning environment, where pupils feel valued. BASICS was one approach that helped to foster these conditions.

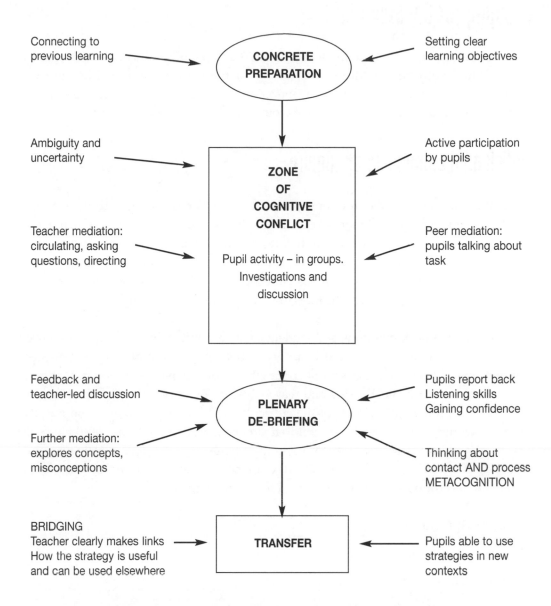

Connecting to previous learning →

Setting clear learning objectives

CONCRETE PREPARATION

Ambiguity and uncertainty →

Active participation by pupils

ZONE OF COGNITIVE CONFLICT

Pupil activity – in groups. Investigations and discussion

Teacher mediation: circulating, asking questions, directing →

Peer mediation: pupils talking about task

Feedback and teacher-led discussion →

Pupils report back Listening skills Gaining confidence

PLENARY DE-BRIEFING

Further mediation: explores concepts, misconceptions →

Thinking about contact AND process METACOGNITION

BRIDGING Teacher clearly makes links How the strategy is useful and can be used elsewhere →

TRANSFER

Pupils able to use strategies in new contexts

CASE is an interesting midpoint between the generic bolt-on course, such as Somerset Thinking Skills or Top Ten Thinking Tactics, and the notion of subject infusion as recommended by Robert Swartz and David Leat. An infusion lesson in science would use Thinking Skills strategies to develop cognitive processes *within* mainstream lessons. CASE really models a STSC approach within the context of a subject but without the usual subject content – it is a sort of 'bolt-on' within the subject.

◆ Philosophy for Children (P4C)

The case for talk has already been made in Chapter 2 and its importance seen throughout this book. Philosophy for Children (P4C) is one of the most significant Thinking for Learning strategies to encourage this collaboration in the classroom so, as part of our examination of some of the approaches, we would like to examine it further here.

Establishing a community of enquiry

If one of the main aims in the development of Thinking for Learning is to help pupils become more independent and more reasonable in their role as learners, then much of the practice needs to focus on strategies that help to do this. It has been our experience over the last five years in Northumberland that the building of a 'Community of Enquiry', as recommended by Matthew Lipman[6] in his Philosophy for Children's approach, can have a major impact upon the learners' attitudes towards school and learning.

Often when teachers ask questions and students answer them, very little thinking takes place. The process is mechanical and contrived – both parties are obeying entrenched conventions based on a covert agreement about what happens in the classroom. Matthew Lipman wanted to stimulate thinking and reasonableness by uncovering and confronting the unclear and problematic aspects of the curriculum. He suggested that a Community of Enquiry would assist this. In it, children are encouraged to think of their own philosophical questions in response to a stimulus. Lines of enquiry are followed and disciplined, focused discussions entail. It demands some flexibility of classroom management and thinking, and students need to be fully engaged.

It encourages students to:

* listen to each other with respect

* build on one another's ideas

* challenge one another to supply reasons

* assist each other in drawing inferences

* identify one another's assumptions

* follow an enquiry where it leads

* conform to a logical pattern of thought.

Community conventions

To run a successful Community of Enquiry everyone needs to abide by some simple conventions. Some teachers shy away from the apparently artificial nature of this – but experience shows that it works.

In a Community of Enquiry:

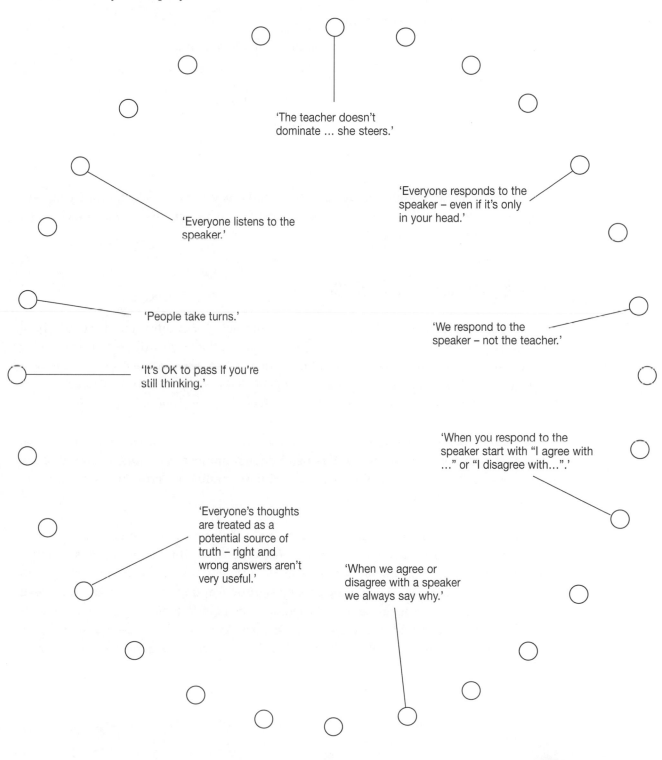

'The teacher doesn't dominate ... she steers.'

'Everyone responds to the speaker – even if it's only in your head.'

'Everyone listens to the speaker.'

'People take turns.'

'We respond to the speaker – not the teacher.'

'It's OK to pass If you're still thinking.'

'When you respond to the speaker start with "I agree with ..." or "I disagree with...".'

'Everyone's thoughts are treated as a potential source of truth – right and wrong answers aren't very useful.'

'When we agree or disagree with a speaker we always say why.'

Thinking for Learning

Successful teachers:

* Choose a suitable stimulus

* Establish the conventions

* Steer the discussion with comments and questions that establish:

    * clarification

        'Are you saying that …'

        'I think you're saying …'

        'Can anyone else say what they think X is saying?'

    * implication

        'So you mean that X would happen next.'

        'If what you say is true, is the reverse also true.'

        'Does that work if …'

Once a healthy community is working the pupils may start to ask the clarifying and implying questions themselves. The teacher can become a silent observer for much of the time (very difficult for some of us).

Running a community of enquiry

Everyone finds their own way of running a community of enquiry that best suits both themselves and their pupils. A common problem is that the teacher finds it difficult to 'let go' of control and is wary of silences of more than a few seconds. Such silences can be a real indication of deep thought about a difficult issue – or, of course, a reluctance to participate. But silences usually resolve themselves if left long enough.

The diagram below illustrates how a Community of Enquiry lesson might be structured. The time spent on each session will depend upon a number of factors, including if the group is used to this method, the complexity of the stimulus and how successful this is in generating questions and discussion.

The Community of Enquiry approach used in the Philosophy for Children programme helps pupils to ask their own questions in response to a stimulus. Using this enquiry-based technique pupils soon learn how to differentiate between interesting and unproductive questions. Whilst they usually start by wanting to ask and answer closed questions like 'What was his name?', 'Where was she going?' their experience soon leads to asking more open and 'philosophical' questions. In answering these questions, they sharpen their reasoning and their ability to justify and evaluate arguments.

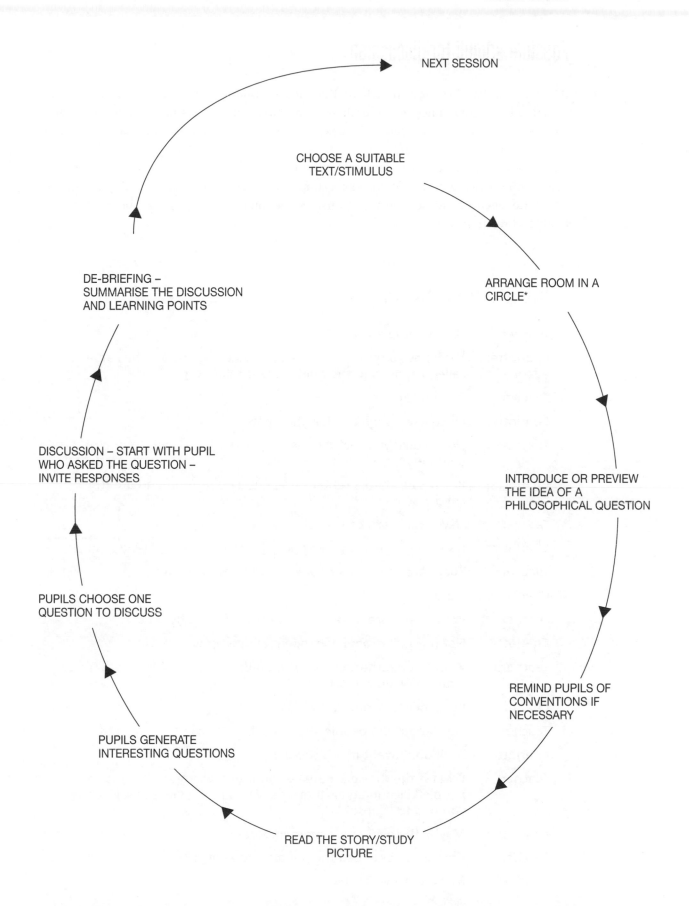

NEXT SESSION

CHOOSE A SUITABLE
TEXT/STIMULUS

ARRANGE ROOM IN A
CIRCLE*

DE-BRIEFING –
SUMMARISE THE DISCUSSION
AND LEARNING POINTS

DISCUSSION – START WITH PUPIL
WHO ASKED THE QUESTION –
INVITE RESPONSES

INTRODUCE OR PREVIEW
THE IDEA OF A
PHILOSOPHICAL QUESTION

PUPILS CHOOSE ONE
QUESTION TO DISCUSS

REMIND PUPILS OF
CONVENTIONS IF
NECESSARY

PUPILS GENERATE
INTERESTING QUESTIONS

READ THE STORY/STUDY
PICTURE

*__Note:__ *This is **not** Circle Time – the intention is to focus on pupils' reasoning skills and develop this
ability to generate interesting and useful questions.*

113

Possible stimuli for discussion

After the initial P4C lesson, where the idea of philosophical questions have been explained and guidelines given, each session afterwards begins by looking at/reading some sort of stimulus. This should be anything that will stimulate thought and questions.

Below is an extract used by James Nottingham with a Year 5 class in the Channel 4 programme *Granny or a Goldfish*. The extract was taken from a real dialogue between Charlotte, aged 6, and her teacher. It raises some interesting questions about ethics, the truth and relationships.

Would You Rather Have a Granny or a Goldfish?

Teacher: Do you have any pets?

Charlotte: Yes. I have a cat and a guinea pig. And a goldfish. The cat is called Zephyr and the guinea pig is called Gip.

Teacher: Do you like them?

Charlotte: Of course. Everyone likes their pets.

Teacher: How would you feel if something awful happened to one of your pets?

Charlotte: Really sad. I had a rabbit once, but a dog got in and ate it. I cried.

Teacher: Have you heard of Africa?

Charlotte: It's a long way away. They have jungles there, and wild animals.

Teacher: There are people there as well. Millions of them.

Charlotte: I know.

Teacher: Would you care if someone in Africa was hit by a bus?

Charlotte: Not much. It probably happens all the time.

Teacher: Would you rather someone you didn't know in Africa was hit by a bus, or your goldfish dies?

Charlotte: I'd rather someone was hit by a bus.

Teacher: How about ten people killed in a bus crash?

Charlotte: I still don't want my fish to die.

Teacher: What if the choice is between your goldfish and a thousand people killed in an earthquake? What if you were magic, and you had to choose?

Charlotte: Maybe the people are more important.

Teacher: What if it's between the people and Zephyr?

Charlotte: No way! I love Zephyr.

Teacher:	What if it's either ten people in Australia killed in a bushfire, or Zephyr hit by a car?
Charlotte:	People I don't know?
Teacher:	Yes. You don't know any of them.
Charlotte:	Then I'd pick Zephyr not to be hit by the car.
Teacher:	What if it's between Zephyr and grandma?
Charlotte:	Um. Grandma's very old. She might die anyway.
Teacher:	What if it's either grandma dies six months before she would have, or Zephyr is hit by a car?
Charlotte:	Are you going to tell grandma what I said?
Teacher:	I don't know. Probably not.
Charlotte:	I think grandma is more important.

Some questions that came up

* Why do people have pets?

* Does everyone have pets?

* What sort of animals make a good pet?

* When you say you are sad, how do you know you are sad?

* Is an animal worth more than a human?

* Does life become less valuable as you grow older?

* Is there a time when it's best not to tell the truth?

. . . and some in response to other stimuli

* Is short-term hardship worth possible long-term benefit?

* Should parents listen to their children?

* Is it right that some people don't have enough to eat?

* Is it possible to think without words?

* What makes a wage fair?

* Are some people worth more than others?

* Are you ever too young to matter?

* Is it ever right to steal?

* What's the difference between telling a lie and keeping a secret?

Asking and choosing questions

The idea is to end with *one* question that is likely to provoke discussion. Initial questions can be generated by whole group, sub-groups or pairs (for example, each group produces three questions – these are shared with whole groups and listed on the board. One question is chosen by debate and/or vote).

What pupils say about P4C

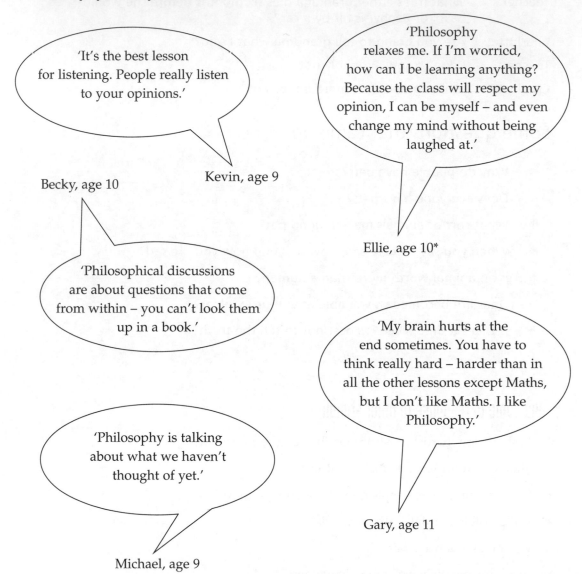

'It's the best lesson for listening. People really listen to your opinions.'

Becky, age 10

Kevin, age 9

'Philosophy relaxes me. If I'm worried, how can I be learning anything? Because the class will respect my opinion, I can be myself – and even change my mind without being laughed at.'

Ellie, age 10*

'Philosophical discussions are about questions that come from within – you can't look them up in a book.'

'My brain hurts at the end sometimes. You have to think really hard – harder than in all the other lessons except Maths, but I don't like Maths. I like Philosophy.'

'Philosophy is talking about what we haven't thought of yet.'

Michael, age 9

Gary, age 11

* *Ellie shows a remarkable capacity for metacognition and interpersonal intelligence. She goes on to say how she performs better in all lessons on days when she has had a Philosophy session.*

Resources for getting started

Robert Fisher[42] has produced a number of books of resources – stories, poems, games for thinking – that are useful for stimulating the discussion. But once you are used to the approach any short story, picture book, fable, poem, etc. can provoke discussion.

For very young children Karin Murris[43] has produced *Storywise: Thinking through Stories* (for other ideas see the Further Reading and Resources section at the end of the book).

Note: *Most of the information provided here has been produced through the work of James Nottingham, a Northumberland teacher now working for the Berwick RAIS Project and a member of SAPERE.[19]*

Stobhillgate First School

Joyce Jenkins of Stobhillgate First School, Northumberland, wanted to assess the impact of P4C on the questioning and reasoning skills of her Year 3 class. Her meticulous study found the following:

* The pupils demonstrated an increased awareness of their own thinking and learning.

* They increasingly made connections to earlier contributions in the discussions, following the logic of arguments and justifying their own beliefs.

* Analysis of vocabulary and understanding of concepts was increasingly demonstrated as the sessions progressed.

* The number of factual, single-issue questions decreased to zero over ten weeks in the sessions, whereas the use of higher level questions doubled.

* The number of factual, single-issue questions decreased by 30 per cent in humanities sessions over the research period, whereas the higher level questions doubled.

* Some pupils' confidence increased, which was commented on by their peers. The more timid children seemed to benefit particularly, as they contributed to the sessions. One even stated, 'I disagree with all of you!' and went on to justify that position.

* Co-operation and collaboration within the group seemed to improve.

A further positive impact of this research was the interest it raised amongst the teacher's colleagues, with more now looking at incorporating P4C into their lessons – possibly the best endorsement of the work done.

Enquiry Drama

Go to Appendix A for more from Tuckswood First

Enquiry Drama (also known as Context or Concept Drama) can be implemented as a useful partner for P4C sessions, where issues discussed in philosophy might then be re-enacted through drama. The staff at Tuckswood First School in Norfolk are currently developing its use in their school

More focused than a general drama lesson, Enquiry Drama seeks to examine issues through exploring the emotions and rationale behind, for example, characters' decisions in stories. The lesson might involve hot-seating a character from a story previously used as a stimulus in a P4C session. This requires a pupil taking on the role of that character and answering questions put forward by others. The child demonstrates empathy, putting aside personal feelings on the specific matter to 'become' someone else, whilst the other children begin to use ever more open and thoughtful questions. A tableau or freeze frame might be an extension of this activity, where characters show their reactions to an event.

Another tool Tuckswood value within this method is 'conscience alley'. In character, a pupil has to walk slowly between two rows of children who form the alleyway. The character may have a decision to make and has opted for one course over another. It is the job of the alley to articulate the pros (on one side) and the cons (on the other side) of that decision. This helps the children to think about the consequences of actions, weigh up arguments and make considered decisions.

In their work so far, Tuckswood found that these methods enhanced the children's creative writing in addition to the benefits outlined above. The Enquiry Drama sessions also had a positive impact on the pupils' self-esteem and on their sense of community.

◆ Other strategies that encourage talk

Living Graphs

Living Graphs are one of the most common and productive types of Thinking for Learning strategies. Graphs, maps and timelines are a very common feature of lessons in many subjects. Pupils often enjoy constructing and analysing graphs, activities that they often find relatively undemanding, but satisfying: a well-drawn graph, perfectly shaded and with some analytical comprehension, looks good! However, when *interpreting* such diagrams, many students struggle to find the sense and meaning behind the data.

Living Graphs develop the real context for the information by personalising it, thus encouraging the students to speculate about how the events, changes or distributions might affect people or environments. This technique involves ambiguity and reasoning. There are often no 'right' answers, only better or worse ones.

How does it work?

The example overleaf is a simple graph showing employment in coal-mines in North East England over a period of time. In this case specific dates and numbers have been omitted so as not to distract attention from the basic task. However, the technique works just as well with more sophisticated and accurate graphs.

Alongside the graph are ten statements about members of the Charlton family. Pupils are asked to place the statements where they think they belong on the graph.

How does talk come into this and how does it help?

1 Initially students work in pairs and agree where to place each statement and why. They have a limited time to do this. At this point they are helping each other to understand what the implications of the statements might be and, therefore, how they might relate to the graph. (The statements can be cut out on card or numbered and the numbers added to the graph.)

2 Each pair joins another and they compare their decisions and reasons. Here there is further clarification about the statements, disagreements to be reconciled and final decisions to be made. Pupils are learning to negotiate, to argue and to justify.

3 After a stated period of time the students are told that they have five minutes to prepare to present their decisions to the rest of the class. They need to justify each decision with a reason.

4 The teacher chooses one group to present their decisions – a blank overhead transparency of the graph is useful for this exercise. The other groups need to listen actively as they will need to find a reason for disagreeing if they wish to do so.

5 The teacher then invites each group to choose one statement, if any, that they consider to be incorrectly positioned. They must give a reason for this.

6 Each group may now be given a few minutes to finalise their positions in the light of what they have heard.

This exercise can be followed up with a writing activity about changing conditions in the coal-mines, using a prepared writing frame or simply used as a review activity.

During this active, and usually fun, lesson students will have practised:

☆ Speculation

☆ Hypothesising

☆ Justification

☆ Articulation

☆ Inferring

☆ Interpreting and analysing.

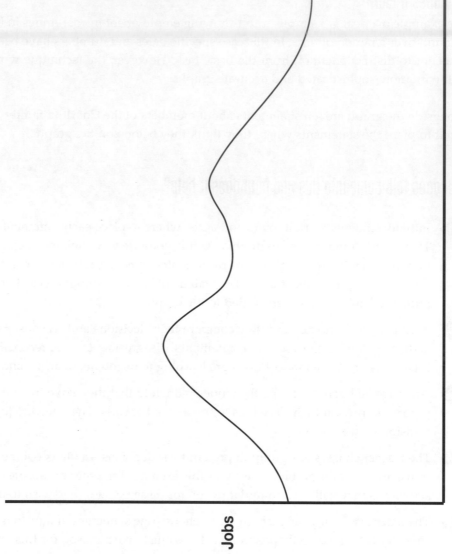

Down the Pit

Jobs

Time

The Charltons — a mining family

★ Robert killed in record pit disaster.

★ Peter Charlton moves to Yorkshire to find work.

★ Cyril says, 'but I'm not trained for any work but mining'.

★ Shortage of canaries in the North East.

★ Tracey Charlton looks after Tiny the pit pony when he is retired.

★ Grandad Charlton says, 'I expect my grandsons to follow me down the pit'.

★ Matthew Charlton learns to operate new machines that make mining easier.

★ Charlton brothers join miners' strike in protest.

★ George is the first Charlton to use the pit-head baths.

★ Sammy Charlton works overtime to meet demands from the new factories.

Classification with Odd One Out

Which of these is the odd one out?

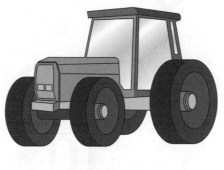

TRACTOR

DUCK

ZEBRA

You probably have an immediate impulse to choose one of them for a perfectly good reason. This is what pupils do. But think for a little longer and you can see how it could be a different odd one out. In fact it could be any of them.

Odd One Out is an excellent warm-up activity at the start of a lesson or a review activity at the end. It can also be built into a more substantial activity to occupy the whole lesson.

Pupils seem to enjoy Odd One Out. It is fun whilst at the same time challenging. It encourages them to play around with their thoughts, looking for other potential solutions, and then articulating these with supporting reasons.

Odd One Out can be used in any subject and with any age group. Which of these is the odd one out?

9   5

10

Again, you can justify any one of them.

When a first school teacher in Northumberland introduced Odd One Out to her 6-year-olds in maths, they simply wanted to get the right answer – and her approval. They were not interested in alternatives. But after a few attempts in different subjects they began to see that it was more interesting to challenge one another's answers and to look for alternative reasons. Now they start by trying to prove each other wrong and look for as many alternative reasons as possible! They have become much more flexible and adventurous in their thinking.

One of the advantages of Odd One Out is that it can be done quickly and orally. There is no need for written responses, although they can come later. Quick thinking and alternatives are what we are looking for at first. Simple recording sheets can be used to encourage pupils to become more precise in their judgements.

This recording sheet encourages pupils to recognise and record both *differences* and *similarities*. Odd One Out can be more sophisticated, especially with older pupils. It may then form a really useful revision exercise that helps:

- ➲ clarify meanings of words
- ➲ develop memory and vocabulary
- ➲ improve classification skills
- ➲ encourage reasoning and language.

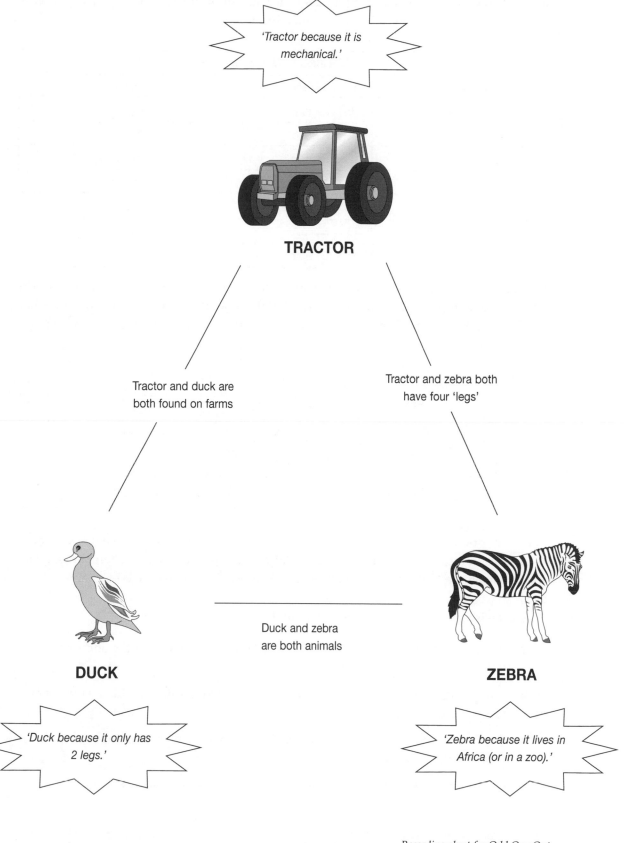

'Tractor because it is mechanical.'

TRACTOR

Tractor and duck are both found on farms

Tractor and zebra both have four 'legs'

DUCK

Duck and zebra are both animals

ZEBRA

'Duck because it only has 2 legs.'

'Zebra because it lives in Africa (or in a zoo).'

Recording sheet for Odd One Out

At this level pupils are given a word list that includes the important terms covered in a topic. Below is one developed by a history teacher in Northumberland. This was used with a Year 11 class at the end of a topic on educational reform.

Education 1750–1850 word list					
1	Laissez-faire	9	Sunday	17	Oxford
2	Public School	10	Factory	18	Rugby
3	Grant	11	Ragged	19	Class
4	Monitorial	12	Religion	20	Standards
5	Dame	13	Boys	21	Behaviour
6	Women	14	Punishment	22	Grammar
7	Elementary	15	Morals	23	Politics
8	Classics	16	By Rote	24	Leadership

Pupils, working in pairs, were then given three sets as below and asked to identify the odd one out. Most importantly they had to say what the other three have in common and what is different about their odd one out. They are developing their ability to group and classify and to explain.

Sets:				
A	4	9	12	15
B	2	7	11	18
C	8	12	16	22

Try these. You may come up with different answers. It does not matter. What does matter is the reasoning behind it. This makes it vital that pupils are asked to share and explain their answers. In that way *misconceptions* can be identified and corrected.

This exercise can then be developed in a number of ways. For example:

❀ Ask pupils to add a further word to each set without changing the odd one out (adding to their classification group).

❀ Ask pupils to make up their own sets of three or four with an odd one out. They can test these on other pupils.

❀ Pupils can sort all the words in the list into a small number of groups – confirming some classifications.

❀ On another topic pupils can compile their own word list and sets.

Note: *It is very important that pupils work collaboratively in pairs/threes so that they have to articulate their reasoning – and develop their own understanding.*

Checking for understanding with Odd One Out

Rachael Michie from Dukes Middle School in Northumberland developed an Odd One Out activity to check pupils' understanding during a CAME thinking maths course. CAME itself was being monitored to study its effect on the pupils' use of mathematical terminology in their Year 7 and Year 8 classes. It was hoped that the programme would produce higher level thinking and reasoning from the groups.

The programme provided opportunities for the pupils to share their ideas with others and explain their reasoning. The teacher found a positive effect on group co-operation and on listening skills. The pupils found it beneficial too. Out of 38 respondents:

- ⌘ 35 enjoyed the lessons

- ⌘ 30 preferred working in a group (five preferred working on their own and three had no preference)

- ⌘ 36 said that they learned something from the lessons

- ⌘ approximately half of them felt that they had worked harder in these lessons, often citing 'being made to think' as the reason. Of the other 50 per cent, many seemed to equate 'hard work' with written evidence. As there is less written work in these lessons, they felt that they had not worked quite as hard.

Despite these largely positive outcomes, it had still been difficult to establish conclusively the pupils' grasp of mathematical terminology after three CAME lessons. Recording the lessons had not been very successful, through poor quality of the reproductions and the sound equipment inhibiting the discussions. The pupils used the terminology when directly questioned by the teacher or when they knew that the teacher was listening. At other times they mainly resorted to communicating their ideas in their own way, but clearly enough for the group with whom they were working.

To resolve the issue, the teacher devised an Odd One Out activity before the fourth CAME lesson. The activity was adapted so that it would become clear if the mathematical terms were understood or not. To this end there was a 'correct' and an 'incorrect' answer, though choices had to be discussed and justified. (See Odd One Out sheet on pages 126–7.)

This activity established that, in most cases, the group understood the terminology. The teacher is now looking at other Thinking for Learning strategies to encourage the students to develop and use mathematical terminology. A further result of this work has been the reflection it has encouraged in the teacher about the teaching strategies 'normally' utilised in maths and the interesting point that several pupils did not view thinking as hard.

The teacher has been pleased with the effect of the CAME lessons on the pupils' higher order thinking, their ability to explain (in their own code) their strategies for working out a maths problem and the enjoyment it has produced. This programme is still being used in addition to the other Thinking for Learning strategies being investigated.

'Odd one out'

Task:

☞ Read the following statements carefully.
☞ Then decide which one is the 'odd one out'.
☞ Once you have decided, shade in the odd one out.
☞ Then explain why you think it is the odd one out.
☞ Share your ideas with the rest of your group and see if you all agree.
☞ As a group, come to an agreement on the correct answer. This may involve you changing your decision.

Metres	Kilometres	Degrees	Miles

1   I think _____ is the odd one out
      because _____

Cuboid	Cylinder	Cone	Sphere

2   I think _____ is the odd one out
      because _____

Diameter	Circumference	Chord	Radius

3   I think _____ is the odd one out
      because _____

Rotation	Reflection	Rotational Symmetry	Clockwise

4   I think _____ is the odd one out
      because _____

Apex	Vertex	Vertices	Edges

5   I think _____ is the odd one out

because _____

Pie Chart	Histogram	Block Graph	Bar Chart

6   I think _____ is the odd one out

because _____

Certain	Maybe	Likely	Impossible

7   I think _____ is the odd one out

because _____

Trapezium	Quadrilateral	Parallelogram	Rectangle

8   I think _____ is the odd one out

because _____

Hundredths	Tens	Units	Hundreds

9   I think _____ is the odd one out

because _____

Polyhedron	Pentahedron	Polygon	Dodecahedron

10   I think _____ is the odd one out

because

Equilateral Triangle	Rectangle	Square	Rhombus

11   I think _____ is the odd one out

because _____

Classification in a science lesson

Julie Howerd of Allendale Middle School, Northumberland, used a Year 7 science lesson on the characteristics of the planets in our solar system to help the pupils learn to sort and classify information.

As in all Thinking for Learning lessons, she began by connecting the learning to what had gone previously, where the pupils had looked at the different planets. She then made explicit the learning objectives: that only Earth is known to support life and that the pupils would also be learning how to sort and classify information.

For the opening activity, she selected four volunteers (two boys, two girls), then asked how the school sorted out the pupils in the school. Correct answers were given (by age and by gender). The teacher then (re)introduced the word 'classification'. Referring to her volunteers, she next asked the class to sort the four into two types of classification. The pupils were asked to do this individually, using 'show-me' boards – white laminated write on/wipe off boards, and were given one minute processing time. When all the boards were held up, she selected pupils to answer and different classifications were established (boy/girl, blonde/dark-haired). For each answer the groupings were physically rearranged, providing visual as well as auditory reference. All answers had to be explained, as did one classification which read 'XX/XY'. Throughout this activity questioning was used to elicit responses and fuller explanations, and humour was used throughout.

This opening, which involved every member of the class, took only a few minutes, clarified the terminology and formed the foundation for the work to follow. At this point, the teacher again made reference to the learning objectives.

The main part of the lesson used data cards on the eight other planets in our solar system. These cards contained pictures and listed information on different aspects of the planets (e.g. mean temperatures, density). The pupils were given one minute to sort them into different classifications according to one piece of information on the cards. Groups were then chosen to explain how they had classified their planets. Temperature was a popular choice in the class, with the planets being sorted into positive and negative mean temperatures. The teacher drew the class's attention to the different strategies used (e.g. selecting a data heading and seeing if there was any way to use that to classify; skimming all the data and selecting an appropriate piece with which to determine classification).

After a brief recap and reference to the learning objectives, the teacher's questions took the pupils further, drawing upon previously learnt content that could be classified (such as what we need to live). This was a good example of near transfer. It was then that the next part was introduced: to draw an alien suitable to live on one of the other planets (given by the teacher). The conditions for life on the planet needed to be considered and the drawing could be annotated. The planet had to remain confidential from the other groups.

After this ten-minute activity, the groups attempted to guess each other's planet based on the information provided by the drawing and the annotation. Reasons for their choices were given.

To finish, the pupils had to consider how the objectives had been met before the teacher summed up the lesson. Several aspects of Thinking for Learning had been utilised, but most importantly process had been made explicit whilst the content was taught.

Sorting pictures

Sorting given information can be a good way of reinforcing and checking understanding of important subject knowledge. It provides the pupils with the opportunity to use their skills to classify that information and then to justify why they opted for those choices.

Glynis Jacobs is a humanities teacher and SENCO at Ryles Park High School, Macclesfield. As part of a lesson about Brazil, she asked the pupils (a Year 8 class with moderate learning difficulties) to sort some carefully selected drawings of scenes from the country into two categories: rich and poor. Her objective was to reinforce the difference between a 'developed' and a 'developing' country, but she wanted the pupils to consider the components that might identify that difference rather than simply being told. As the pupils worked on the task, she took on the role of mediator, circulating and interacting with them, using questions and providing information to direct their thinking. The activity should also have assisted their recall of the information.

Thoughtful, open questioning strategies had been used earlier as part of determining the connection between the last lesson, where they had discussed the differences between developed and developing countries, and this one. They would be used again in a later lesson when the pupils would have to provide reasons for why they chose to place a picture in either the 'rich' or the 'poor' category. This feedback would involve encouraging the fullest possible answers from individuals and summaries from the teacher to ensure that the information was clear to the rest of the class. Again, this is a form of mediation. Inviting pupils to articulate their deliberations helps the teacher to ascertain whether the objectives have been achieved or not. Links could then be reinforced between the work they have been doing on Brazil and developing/developed nations, explaining again how the activity had assisted their learning in the subject. The possibility of transfer is built in when the use of the activity is explained to them and other situations discussed where sorting might be used to help their learning.

The follow-on work will concentrate on their writing. A 'template' will be used to prompt the pupils towards crafting a well-written piece, with statements on the classroom walls reminding them of what is important for written work, such as keeping to the point of the question. The activity of sorting, however, could also be used as a brief beginning or as a review of a lesson.

Organising ideas using concept maps

This is where the key words/concepts are laid out for a particular subject. Links are then drawn between the different words/phrases and their connections explained. Pupils need to be able to classify information and then to show the relationships between the various items. A simple concept map might be like the one overleaf, mapping out the associations between the characters in *Great Expectations*.

Characters in Great Expectations

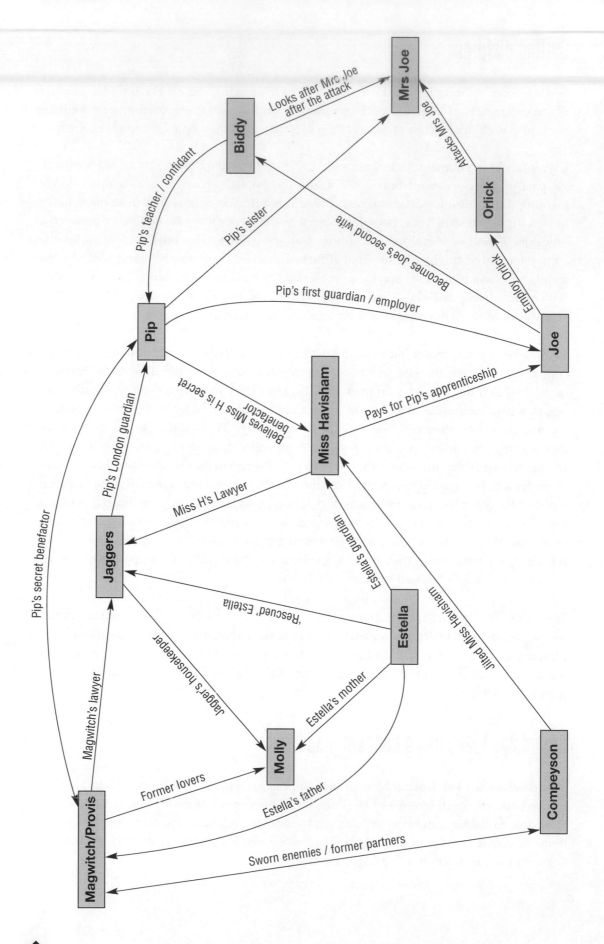

A humanities teacher, Claire Harbottle, at Haydon Bridge High School in Northumberland found that concept maps helped to raise self-esteem and motivation levels, as well as improving attainment. They were used in three lessons with a poorly motivated mixed ability Year 9 class. She observed that concept maps:

* Helped those who normally did not participate in class to join in, using the vocabulary in front of them and so lifting their confidence.

* Encouraged the pupils to ask and answer more questions, as they verbalised their efforts.

* Were especially popular when constructed in groups. Discussion ensued from individuals having to justify their contributions.

* Highlighted areas for development, such as historical and thinking terminology.

Although, she states, it is impossible to isolate concept mapping as the sole reason for improvement, she found that in written work over three lessons when measured against specified criteria (analysis and inference, structure and relevance, explanation and the language of discourse):

* 20 per cent of pupils improved by one level in three or more of the criteria.

* 50 per cent of pupils improved by one level in two or more of the criteria.

* 24 per cent of pupils improved by one level in one of the criterion, of which the most common area was improved analysis and inference.

* For 26 per cent of the pupils there was no measurable change in attainment.

'Concept mapping gets you to think more and not just accept someone else's opinion in a textbook.'

Year 9 pupil

'I don't say anything in case I get it wrong. In concept mapping lessons there wasn't a right answer and this gave me more confidence to think and try more. Instead of one answer the discussion helped me to think of three or four.'

Year 9 pupil

An outline of the sequence of three lessons is reproduced below.

 Go to page 132

 Go to page 139

 Go to page 142

 Go to page 121

Lesson sequence	Thinking Skills activities used to generate concepts	Nature of Concept Map	Follow up lesson outcome
1	**Reading Photographs** depicting images of WWI life in the trenches. **Story Telling** using soldiers' letters.	Produced **individually** with key words associated with living conditions and soldiers' feelings.	Piece of creative writing (newspaper article) – *Recollections of a Veteran.*
2	**Mystery** based on the experiences of a Jewish family in Hitler's Germany.	Produced **in pairs** with keywords associated with persecution of the Jews and feelings of the victims.	Piece of creative writing (diary) – *Living through the Holocaust.*
3	Concept Cartoons,[48] **Odd One Out** and Reading Photographs comparing lifestyles of North American Indians and the white man.	Produced **in groups of four** with keywords associated with lifestyles.	Causation essay – *Why was there conflict between the Indian and the White Man?*

131

Reading photographs: an approach to generating pupil questions

Teachers often use photographs as a way of introducing content in English, geography, science, modern foreign languages, etc. Most frequently we concentrate on pictures as description and first-hand evidence. This is fine, but there is also tremendous potential for using photographs to generate questions and discussion.

Method one: using sets of photographs to introduce a topic and generate general enquiry questions

This is a good activity for making connections, comparing and contrasting. Sets of photographs of historical periods (for example, Victorians/Edwardian England/First or Second World War/Social Change in the twentieth century) or geographical areas can be used. The suggested groups of photographs do not even need to be used for those particular subjects. For example, pictures from the two world wars could be used to introduce war poetry. In pairs or groups pupils can be asked to:

1 Arrange photographs into pairs and then ask, 'What have these photographs got in common?'

2 Pairs of pupils then join up and explain why they have linked their two photographs together. Listening pairs are encouraged to ask questions about the photographs.

Method two: using photographs to raise issues and explore contexts

Photographs of exotic tourist locations or of urban crime can prompt questions such as:

- 'Who took this photograph?'

- 'What was their reason for taking it?'

- 'What do you think the people in the picture thought about their photographs being taken?'

- 'What could this photograph be used for?'

- 'Is the photograph natural or posed?'

Once pupils are introduced to this type of question they become much more inquisitive, speculative and interested in the topic.

Method three: uncovering photographs

Photographs can be uncovered gradually, or covered with cut-out windows. Some photographs are very useful for this, especially where a number of people or different activities are included in the scene. Pupils are asked to:

1. comment on what they can see at each stage.

2. speculate about what they think will come next.

3. ask questions about what they see.

The photograph of a Victorian Street scene overleaf illustrates this well. Pupils have asked:

* 'Did they have cameras in those days?'

* 'What is that man taking a picture of?'

* 'Are those his children?'

* 'Isn't it dangerous to play in the street?'

* 'Are they all brothers and sisters?'

* 'What are they playing?'

Method four: transforming observation into questions

1. Ask the pupils to identify between three and five objects or people in the photograph.

2. Pupils give each of these a name (noun).

3. Pupils add adjectives and verbs to the noun to create a descriptive sentence.

4. The sentence is transformed into a question by adding why, who, what, where, etc.

Working together: memory maps

One of the key features of Thinking for Learning strategies is that they encourage and develop collaborative skills and attitudes. And yet we often hear teachers grumbling that pupils will not work together and that group work is impossible because they will not co-operate or stay on task.

Memory maps (or maps from memory) are worth trying with any pupils, but especially those who often find collaborative work difficult. It is easy to set up, injects a sense of urgency and pace, is an excellent technique for developing memory skills and close observation, and is fun when done in a group.

Whilst we call this technique 'memory *maps*' it can be used with any visual material. It is noticeable that pupils tend to find memorising symbols and pictorial information much easier than memorising text. Is it easier for them to memorise information if they work as a group rather than if they work individually? There is no clear answer to that but it is

Victorian street photo
Reproduced by permission of the Beamish Museum, Co Durham

apparent that pupils themselves recognise the benefits of working together to develop a wider range of strategies than they could on their own.

How does it work?

There are a few variations on the central strategy. You can probably devise more of your own. Pupils seem to work best in groups of between three and five on this exercise. The challenge is to reproduce the map/diagram as accurately as possible. The maps will be judged according to the amount and accuracy of material successfully recorded.

1 Each group has a sheet of plain paper and a set of coloured pencils.

2 Pupils take turns to come to the centre of the room where the teacher shows them the map for ten seconds.

3 Pupils return to their group and record as much as they can remember. They can talk to the rest of the group as they do so.

4 Each pupil in turn comes out to view the map for ten seconds and returns to add detail to the group map.

5 The number of turns pupils are given depends upon the time available and the complexity of the original.

6 Pupils have a final two minutes to add any further detail to their map.

7 Each group pins up their map and explains how they organised the task and what they found easiest/hardest to remember.

8 De-briefing by the teacher is the most valuable part of the exercise. Try to get the pupils to identify and explain the strategies they used. Would they use these again? Or would they borrow from another groups' ideas? If they repeated the exercise with a new stimulus next week, would they perform better using the strategies they have identified from the start?

Is working as a group more effective than working alone? (Try it!)

Also the benefits of using this technique have been noted in the classroom. When asked to reproduce a map three weeks later, pupils who used the memory map technique remembered significantly more than their peers who had been given the map to copy and told to learn it.

What sorts of strategies emerge?

Some groups immediately organise and begin to develop strategies for optimising time and skills available. Others flounder for a while and gradually improve.

Commonly observed strategies include:

✿ If there is a border or grid, copy that first as a frame of reference. Experienced groups may impose a grid on the map – even when there is not one!

✿ Apportion responsibility for different parts of the map – top right/bottom left/grid square A1, etc.

✿ With coloured images different pupils look for different colours.

✿ Start from the middle and work out.

✿ 'You remember the words, I'll get the picture.'

✿ Everyone focuses on one part of the diagram until its finished.

Variations

The first time we used this strategy there was a standard format, as described above. Pupils worked in groups of between three and five and took turns to visit the stimulus. Since then other variations have arisen. For example:

✪ As above *but* when the pupil returns to the group, they have to describe what they have seen whilst someone else draws it. (More difficult, challenges ability to communicate.)

✪ Only one pupil is nominated to visit the map, the rest of the group give instructions about what to look for.

✪ The stimulus/map is projected on an OHP or slide projector for periods of 10 seconds. Pupils stay seated and work co-operatively to recall the image. In this case they all see it at once. This works best in pairs, or at most in groups of three.

Stimulus

This can be anything: a map in history or geography, a systems diagram in science or maths, a block diagram, a poem, even an artefact in RE!

An example is included on the opposite page – it could be coloured.

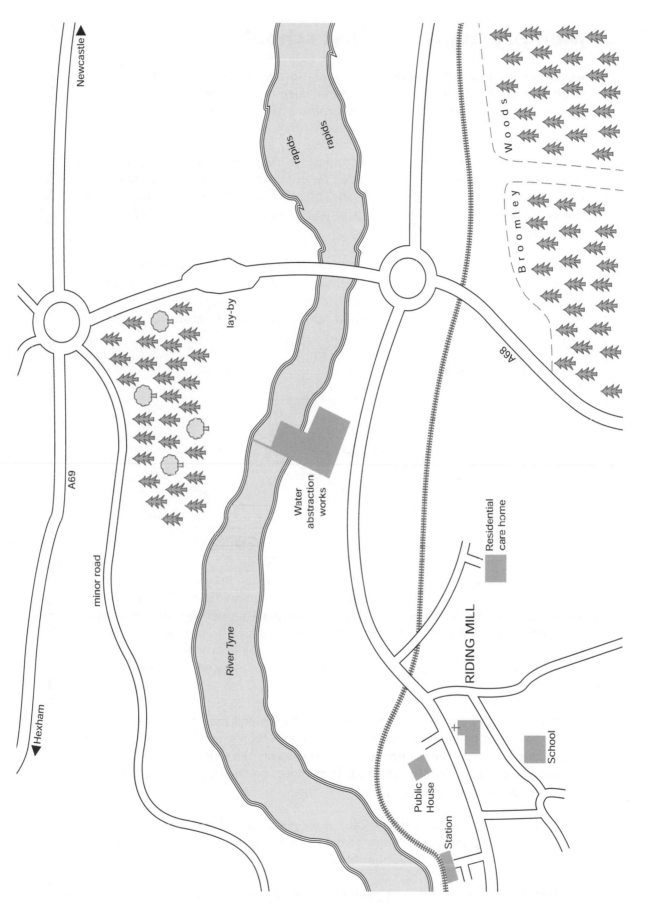

A map to memorise

Memory maps in a first school

Alison Hawkins from Allendale First School, Northumberland, looked at the strategies her Year 2 and 3 pupils used in a 'memory map' activity for geography. As in many Thinking for Learning activities the emphasis was in working collaboratively to achieve a successful outcome.

The task was to remember a country's name, its flag and its capital city. The mixture of writing and picture provided an opportunity for all ability levels to participate whilst also covering relevant content and connecting to literacy. The last two of the six country groupings to be remembered were more difficult in name and unfamiliarity with the flag.

The groups were given a sheet of A3 paper divided into six sections, one for each country/flag/capital city combination. The information to be memorised was hidden from the rest of the class, allowing only one pupil per group to study it at any one time. They each had ten seconds before returning to the others.

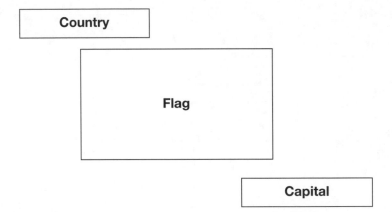

Some of the pupils returned to their groups and began drawing or writing on their own, whereas others questioned the returnee immediately. The questions were mainly a bombardment, though some were a little gentler. This seemed to be a reflection of the urge of most pupils to be involved. In one group, one of the girls took over, acting as scribe and translating the instructions from the others as they returned, an interesting and more complicated dimension to the activity.

Mainly, it was the written information that was remembered first. When they began the flags, they began with the outline and then moved on to the design. Interestingly, one of the groups negotiated the way the stripes ran on one flag, showing good team decision making. The colours on the flags were often harder to remember within its design.

As a follow-up to this activity, the class was tested the following week on the countries and capital cities. This informal testing is a good way of revisiting the content for retention in the longer term.

Working together: sequencing

Sequencing information in a group is another method of encouraging children to work together productively. If each group has to agree an order for the information provided, then any disagreements within the group need to be resolved through articulating and justifying personal opinions. In this way not only have the individual pupils arrived at their own 'answer', but they also need to listen to other views and reassess their own ideas, working collaboratively to negotiate an outcome acceptable to all.

The plan from one such lesson given by Lynn Johnston of Allendale First School, Northumberland is shown in Appendix B1. It involved the children sequencing different toys along a simple timeline ('past…present') and then giving reasons for their decisions. The pictures were a model of a butcher's shop, a Lego helicopter, a clockwork Mickey Mouse toy, a stagecoach and a Meccano model of a crane.

As expected there was a range of 'answers', none of which was deemed 'correct' or 'incorrect'. The teacher was interested in the children's processing. What had made them make that particular choice? These responses highlighted some astute observations, such as noticing that the butcher was wearing a top hat (so it should be earlier in the sequence), that helicopters were a relatively recent form of transport (the latest toy in most selections), the boy playing with one toy was in modern clothes and Mickey Mouse had a barrow cart, which you do not see these days.

Encouraging listening and practising memory techniques through story telling

Some Year 9 pupils were spending just one lesson on volcanic activity, having spent much longer studying earthquakes.[14] The teacher wanted to give them a memorable lesson so that the best use was made of limited time. She decided to use the 'Story Telling' technique – not as simple as it sounds and certainly not about pupils passively listening to a story.

Pupils are divided into three groups: 1s, 2s and 3s. Then the following takes place:

1. The 2s and 3s leave the room and are given a brief task (for example, locating volcanoes on a world map) under supervision.

2. The 1s are told that the teacher is going to read/tell them a story about a volcanic eruption and its consequences. Their task is to remember the story so that they can retell it to the 2s who will have to retell it to the 3s. They must *listen* and are not allowed to take notes.

3. After hearing the story the 1s have a few minutes to discuss the story amongst themselves (in pairs) and are allowed to ask one question each about the story.

4. The 2s are brought in. *Either* the 1s pair up with a 2 and retell the story *or* the whole group of 1s (or pairs/threes) retell to a similar size group. Again the 2s listen without taking notes. Then they can ask a few questions.

5 Then the 3s come in (the 1s may be asked to leave or just observe) and the process is repeated.

6 Finally the 3s retell the story to the whole class. If the class have listened well and used sensible strategies they usually remember a lot of the story.

When the teacher de-briefed the class using questions such as 'How did you try to remember?' 'Do people remember things in different ways?' and 'Can we all use these skills?', the pupils were able to identify these strategies:

★ Remembering the story as a picture (visualising).

★ Remembering the plot not the details (for example, names of characters/places – these 'clog-up' the brain).

★ Remembering the story as a sequence or chain.

★ Turning the story into a map or diagram in their mind.

★ Inventing a title or moral for the story to give it meaning or point.

They then identified the following skills they had used:

♠ listening

♠ visualising

♠ selecting information

♠ sequencing

♠ discussing

♠ questioning

♠ co-operating

♠ communicating

♠ explaining

♠ having confidence.

De-briefing: the Bangladesh Floods Mystery

'Mysteries' are one of the most commonly used and powerful strategies in the Thinking for Learning classroom. As a rule, pupils find them motivating and challenging. Pupil talk and collaboration are unavoidable and many learning skills can be developed.

In a Mystery pupils are given one or two key questions to answer and a bank of statements that provide evidence, clues and often red herrings. What these statements never do is give a clear, undeniable answer to the question. The answer has to be deduced and constructed by the pupils. The types of thinking involved can include:

- ❖ classification
- ❖ cause and effect
- ❖ sequencing
- ❖ speculation
- ❖ synthesis
- ❖ hypothesising.

In 1996 SCAA (the old Schools Curriculum Assessment Authority – later absorbed by QCA) published a series of optional tasks for Key Stage 3 geography, which included the Kobe Earthquake Mystery. In 2000 the National Literacy Strategy released a Key Stage 3 training video[53] that included a geography lesson taught by Douglas Greig at Thomas Tallis School in Greenwich in which pupils used the Bangladesh Floods Mystery to establish their geographical knowledge and their literacy skills. When we look at the planning (see pages 142–5), we can see the clear intention to include de-briefing in the column headed 'Teacher's Activities', that is:

 In Mustafa's Story – 'to listen to and use the students as a learning resource'.

 In the mystery – 'to guide their thinking and to model new ideas and generalisation ... through open-ended questions', 'whole class discussion and feedback sessions'.

Whilst teachers recognise the value of de-briefing about the learning process – the 'how' of learning rather than the 'what have we learned' – many still find it difficult to fit in the time. And yet both pupils and teachers agree on the importance of regular talk about learning.

If pupils are to become 'Intentional Learners' ('intentionality' is discussed on page 48), then de-briefing and metacognition must be at the centre of the learning process so that pupils can genuinely develop their thinking and learning skills.

De-briefing: some of the key points

- ☆ Teachers need to make time for de-briefing – to plan this time into their lessons and to plan the debriefing process itself.

- ☆ De-briefing is most effective if learning objectives are clear and pupils are aware of them.

- ☆ De-briefing becomes easier as pupils develop a 'Thinking Vocabulary'. This needs to be planned for and developed over time.

- ☆ Paired or group work needs to be carefully structured and paced so that the emphasis is largely on thinking and learning rather than on social processes.

141

☆ De-briefing needs to explore explicitly the potential for transfer if this is to happen.

☆ Formative, analytical assessment is aided by skilful be-briefing.

☆ Teachers need to allow pupils adequate 'processing time' (often silence) in response to questions and to encourage them to use this time for reflection. It may be useful to encourage pupils to develop their answers.

☆ De-briefing is most effective, and taken seriously by pupils, when a consistent approach is taken by staff.

☆ For de-briefing to be used effectively and frequently, the strategies used must be varied, just as they are in the main activities of the lesson.

☆ De-briefing is a key feature of intentional learning.

☆ If pupils see themselves merely as passive recipients of teaching, as 'little jugs' to be filled, they are unlikely to participate in de-briefing activities.

☆ All Thinking for Learning activities are dependent upon there being a conducive ethos where pupils feel safe, are able to take risks and are not afraid of making mistakes.

The Bangladesh Floods Mystery

We are pleased to be able to include Douglas Greig's Bangladesh Floods Mystery, which is reproduced here with kind permission from Douglas. This mystery, listed on the Key Stage 3 training video as 'Lesson 5 Douglas – Floods', provides an excellent example of Thinking Skills in action. You are recommended to watch it if you also want to see the potential benefits of using mysteries first hand. Your Literacy Co-ordinator should have a copy.

The Bangladesh Floods of 1998

Lesson Content	Literacy Element	Students' Activities	Teacher's Activities	Research
1 Mustafa's Story • An introductory activity which aims to establish the location and events of the Bangladesh Flood of 1998. • The core activity is to listen to the story of Mustafa, a young Bangladeshi boy and to write down important events for the oral presentation. • Taking notes and sequencing the narrative and contextual elements of the story. • To reflect on how people remember and take notes from oral and visual presentations. **Geography National Curriculum** • Describing the effects of flooding on different groups of people. • Developing an understanding of life in an LEDC context. • To study how the effects of such a natural disaster and human responses to them differ in countries at different levels of economic development. • To develop an extended geographical vocabulary within an applied context. • To select secondary sources of information including text and photographs.	• Listening to an oral presentation. Selecting and noting key ideas and notes down. • To group these ideas together to distinguish different categories within the narrative. • Group listening to a presentation made by the teacher. • To reflect on how we remember ideas and important events to take down in notes. • To understand that all texts follow a sequence and to understand and to make sense of this sequence is the key to making notes.	1 Listen to oral presentation once, and write down any important facts, ideas and events within the story. 2 To reflect upon how they did this, to draw up groups and categories for making sense of the narrative and non-factional content of the story. To do this through oral feedback to the rest of the group. 3 To listen to the story for a second time and use these strategies explicitly to take down notes and ideas. To use the new categories and groups that they drew up to make sense of the content. 4 A good homework activity from this lesson is to get the student's to select the photographs out of the nine to choose from that they would use to make a photostory about the floods.	1 To establish the aims of the lesson clearly and to make the literacy element of the lesson explicit to the students. 2 To read the story to the students in an animated fashion so as to involve them in the narrative, and to motivate them to listen. 3 To facilitate and model the formation of ideas about how we learn and how note taking can become more effective. 4 To listen and use the students as a learning resource.	• Story 'Mustafa's Story'. • Photographs for the photostory

Lesson Content	Literacy Element	Students' Activities	Teacher's Activities	Research
2 The Bangladesh Floods Mystery Game • Posing of a mystery/question that the students are then involved in solving and explaining in pairs or small groups. • To extract data and classify it in order to select and mobilise certain aspects of it to answer a particular question. • Talking to learn. • Reading to learn. • Recording written generalisations based upon oral work. • Development of critical thinking skills. **Geography National Curriculum** • Explaining the causes and impacts of floods. • To explain the movements of goods and people. • To explain that processes operating at different scales can bring about change in places. • Developing an understanding of life in an LEDC context. • To study how the effects of such a natural disaster and human responses to them differ in countries at different levels of economic development. • To explain the interrelationships between people and the environment. • To establish a sequence of investigation and draw substantial conclusions.	• Classifying. • Summarising. • Questioning. • Predicting. • Prioritisation. • Reading and rereading. • Development of thinking through talking. • Oral feedback in a variety of contexts and forums (public and private). • To make sense of written texts through oral discussion and written generalisation. • To engage in the active construction of meaning through reading, writing, speaking and listening. • To mirror one experience of reading that students have in the real world: small amounts of text about dramatic events.	1 Students made familiar with the Mystery Game as a DART, with the aims of the task. 2 Lay out the cards and begin to read them for the first time. 3 Group off useful and irrelevant pieces of information in relation to the task they have to answer. 4 Students should then be encouraged to group the information into different categories such as human causes, natural causes, background causes, trigger causes, effects on people, health, water, housing, work, wealth. These are but a few of many possibilities. A key element of progression within the task is to make links between these various groups. 5 At regular intervals the students should stop in their enquiry and feedback their findings to the whole group. After these sessions they should note their findings in the grids they have been given. This is an important element that allows them to formulate, evaluate and reformulate their ideas. 6 To come up with a final generalisation about the issue in the mystery game. 7 To reflect upon how and what they have learned.	1 To establish the aims of the lesson clearly and to make the literacy element of the lesson explicit to the students. 2 To split the class into suitable and manageable groupings for the task. 3 The teacher must pose the question clearly at the beginning of the lesson. Her/his role then becomes to monitor the progress of the students, to guide their thinking and to model new ideas and generalisations. This should be done through open-ended questions – ones that do not have one fixed answer. 4 The teacher may have to intervene with some groups – to give them pointers as to how they can use some cards and discard others. 5 At about 10 minute intervals the teacher should hold whole class discussions and feedback sessions. These are crucial to the development of thinking and for the demonstration of successful lines of enquiry to those who might be struggling. Again open-ended questions should be used to draw out groups and links between the groups.	• Bangladesh Flood Mystery Game (15 × packs of 36 laminated cards). • Note taking grid and instructions.

Lesson Content	Literacy Element	Students' Activities	Teacher's Activities	Research
3 **Why did the flood of 1998 have such a big effect on Bangladesh?** • To consolidate the previous learning and apply this to the presentation of written conclusion to the above question. • To produce an extended piece of writing drawing conclusions about the causes and effects of flooding in a LEDC. **Geography National Curriculum** • Explaining the causes and impacts of floods. • To explain the movements of goods and people. • To explain that processes operating at different scales can bring about change in places. • Developing an understanding of life in an LEDC context. • To study how the effects of such a natural disaster and human responses to them differ in countries at different levels of economic development. • To explain the interrelationships between people and the environment. • To establish a sequence of investigation and draw substantiated conclusions.	• To present findings in an extended and structured piece of writing that demonstrates an understanding of the sequence of a text and to the vocabulary appropriate for this topic. • Use of subject specific vocabulary. • Writing for a particular purpose. • Writing independently. • To develop an understanding of how non-fiction texts operate. • To plan a piece of non-fiction writing (extension task).	1 Use of the cards and notes that they have used in the previous lesson to write a conclusion to a broader and more 'objective' question. This is to be in the form of a photostory using the pictures they were previously given. 2 Students can use the writing frames which are differentiated at different levels to support and scaffold their learning. The most able students should be challenged to produce their own writing frame (or plan in child speak) for how they will answer the question.	1 To decide which students should complete which activity and thus to assess which writing frame will best suit the needs of individual students. 2 To monitor and support the process of writing for some students, providing different levels of structure where appropriate. 3 To ensure that the least able do not simply copy information. Students will need support in developing reasoning and causation in their writing if they are to develop anything more than a descriptive approach.	• Writing Frames 'Why did the flood of 1998 have such a big effect on Bangladesh?' These are available at different levels of difficulty.

How do river floods affect people?

Imagine that your house gets flooded with water. It has covered the floor up to a depth of 50cm. All of the homes in your neighbourhood are in the same position.

1 Make a list of all the damage that might be done by the water, both inside and outside the house.

2 If the flood carries on for a week, what problems would this create for you and your family? Make another list of these problems.

3 If you received a warning that the flood was going to happen one hour beforehand, what would you and your, family do to reduce the damage? Who would you contact to help you?

4 When the flood has happened what would you expect the fire and ambulance service to do?

5 What would you want the local council and the national government to do?

6 Once you moved back into your house after the flood, what would you do make the risk of damage from a flood less in the future'?

Mustafa's story

Mustafa woke up early on the Tuesday morning in time to get himself ready for school. He knows he's lucky as none of his other brothers and sisters are going to school at the moment, but at the same time he always wishes he didn't have to get up so early. His school is about 2 miles away from his home across the flat flood plain of the River Ganges. Bangladesh where Mustafa lives is a very flat place as it is mostly made up of the delta of three rivers. That's the area of land that the rivers make when they reach the sea and dump off the mud and silt that they are carrying because they slow down in the ocean. Gradually this dumped material builds up into new land, and is why most of Mustafa's country is under 100m high.

It had been raining for three days. In fact since April it had rained much more than it usually would, and it had got really bad when the rainy season started in June. Now in September, all of this rain meant that the rivers and streams near where Mustafa lived were really full and some had flooded. Mustafa hated the rain. It meant his walk to school would be uncomfortable and that he and his friends wouldn't be able to play outside.

He switched on the radio to try and find something to listen to while he got ready. All of a sudden he heard a lady's voice as he was turning the dial. She was speaking quite quickly and in the background you could hear lots of people moving, shouting and screaming. The lady continued to speak.

'I'm here in Mirpur a district of Dhaka our capital city. I'm standing on one of the only roads out of the city that is left open as hundreds and thousands of people run away from the flood waters that are covering the land and buildings in Mirpur.

To date 75% of Bangladesh is under the flood water. 30,000 villages have disappeared or been destroyed. 30 million people have been left homeless. On top of this people rely on the land to grow food and to earn a living. With 1 million hectares of land under water, most of the farming has had to stop because the crops and animals are often drowned under the water. This also means that many thousands of people are in danger of losing their only way of earning a living.'

Mustafa was putting his shirt on as the lady on the radio spoke. When she got to this point he stopped. His shirt was half on and half off. Mirpur. That's where his Uncle and Aunt and their children lived. Gradually, a real sense of fear dawned on Mustafa. His Uncle, Aunt and cousins were probably leaving their home right then. They would be running around the house desperately trying to grab what they could. What would they leave? What would they take? What would they do? Where would they go? Mustafa listened on to the lady on the radio.

'The biggest worry now is about the spread of diseases. All over the country 800 people have died. Only a few of these have drowned. Most have died from illnesses such as diarrhoea which are spread because people can't eat properly and because it is really difficult to get clean drinking water because of the floods. Another disease, Malaria, is spreading quickly. This is because it is spread by mosquitoes which infect people when they bite them to suck their blood as a quick meal. Mosquitoes love warm and damp conditions, two things that it definitely has been during the floods. People's crops are rotting in the fields they were planted in, which are now covered in water. The food and income of many families has just disappeared overnight. With 30 million people homeless the government now faces the problem of finding enough food, clean water and shelter for all these people. In a less developed and poor country like Bangladesh which is overcrowded, people's way of life is too fragile to be able to deal with a natural disaster like this one. One mistake and a whole family can find itself ruined overnight. A solution must be found to this huge human problem before more people join the already high death toll.'

Mustafa could not believe it. He knew that it had been wet. Very wet. Loads of rain had fallen and the rivers around his village were high. But this was bad. Really bad. He knew this wasn't going to be an ordinary day. He ran outside and loudly called out his father's name. Today, school could wait.

There are two families to look at in this mystery – the Hossain family and the Chowdury family who both live in Dhaka, the capital of Bangladesh. Four days after the floods began, one of these families had to leave their home and move away. Your task is to find out who decided to move and why this happened.

Names: _____

First thoughts and findings: _____

_____

_____

_____

_____

_____

_____

Further thoughts and findings: _____

_____

_____

_____

_____

_____

_____

_____

_____

Conclusion: _____

_____

_____

_____

_____

_____

_____

_____

_____

The flood meant that the sewage system was broken which polluted the water which people use for cooking and drinking.	People in Dhaka could not boil their water because most of them did not have the wood or fuel to make fires.
With much less food around, food prices in Dhaka have risen massively.	Mr Hossain's cousin Nayeem lives in a village north of Dhaka on higher ground which has not been affected by the flood. There was food and shelter there.
The Hossains spent three days living on top of their house when the floods hit Mirpur in late August.	Mr and Mrs Hossain decided to only eat one meal a day after the flood happened to try and save food.
Trees and forests soak up rain. Rainwater hitting bare ground runs off into rivers and streams very quickly and increases the risk of rivers flooding.	In August the government issued a warning that people should boil their water for 10 minutes so that it was safe to drink.
Three times more rain fell over Bangladesh in the Monsoon period from April to September 1998 than normal.	Bangladesh is one of the poorest countries in the world. The average income for each person in one year is US$l,330. In the UK it is US$21,200.
Much of the rice and other food crops has rotted in the fields where it was growing, drowned under the flood water .	As the population of Bangladesh has grown, people have built more towns and roads. These don't absorb water when it rains, and so the rivers in Bangladesh fill up more quickly and flood more easily.
Every year in Bangladesh the rivers flood, but this was the worst for ten years.	The flood hit Dhaka in late August after a month of flooding in northern parts of the country. However, people did not expect it to have such a large effect .
Mr and Mrs Hossain live in a low-lying area of Dhaka called Mirpur which is next to the flood plain of the river.	In Bangladesh, families look after other family members who are in need of help or money.
In Dhaka people could not get to the hospitals and doctors easily because of the destruction of roads and buildings. Many families were trapped in or on top of their houses for many days.	Mr Hossain's cousin Nayeem runs a health centre in the village where he lives.

Mystery game cards

The lack of clean water has meant that diarrhoea has become a very large problem. 100,000 people were reported suffering from it all over Bangladesh, and 100 people have died.	Human beings are changing the world's climate by putting more Carbon Dioxide into the atmosphere. This means that more heat from the sun is absorbed which creates Global Warming.
Mosquitoes breed well in warm and wet conditions.	Mr and Mrs Chowdury live in a wealthy part of Dhaka which is on high ground.
The Chowdury's could not get into work but their house was safe from the flood waters.	Two days after their house was flooded the Hossain's youngest child caught diarrhoea and their oldest son had the symptoms of malaria.
The Chowdury's were lucky to have enough savings to be able to buy the food and fuel they needed.	20% of the population of Bangladesh is in danger of starving because they cannot get enough food to eat as a result of the flooding.
In the Himalayan mountains in Nepal, India and China, many forests have been cut down to provide wood for construction and export, as well as land for farming.	Bangladesh has a population density of 989 people per square kilometre.
On the fourth day after the flood began in Dhaka, the Hossain family decided to leave the city and go to stay with Mr Hossain's cousin in a village north of Dhaka.	Mr and Mrs Chowdury had lots of savings which they could use to get them through these hard times.
Bangladesh is located on the low and flat area of land at the end of two large rivers – the Ganges and the Bhramaputra. This area is called a delta, and the sources of these rivers are in the Himalaya mountains.	Many people have died from malaria, which is spread by mosquitoes when they bite people to feed on their blood.
Global warming has meant that the weather in certain places has become either wetter or drier.	The Hossains had few savings and quickly found themselves with no way of earning money or rebuilding their home.
Mr Hossain works in the food market and bazaar in Mirpur, and Mrs Hossain works in a rice packing factory.	30 million people all over Bangladesh were made homeless by this flood.

Mystery game cards

Why did the flood of 1998 have such a big effect in Bangladesh?

Task:

Your task is to produce a photostory which answers the above question using the photographs that you have been given. You will use the photos as the different screen shots, and will then write the words that the narrator would say over the top to tell the story.

You will need to give some background as to where Bangladesh is, and to explain what the causes and effects of the flooding were. After that you must then answer the above questions using all the information at your fingertips to come to your own conclusion. You must use at least five of the photographs to tell your story, and must think carefully about what is in your picture and what you are writing for the narrator to say.

Writing Frame:

Introduction:

In this section you will need to introduce where you are going to write about and some clues as to what has happened there. So you will need to explain where Bangladesh is and some factual data about the flood that happened in 1998.

Causes of the Flood:

You will now need to explain how the fold was caused. In your writing you will need to group different causes together, such as weather, human activity, landscape of Bangladesh. To produce an excellent piece of geography in this section you need to draw links between these different causes to explain how one cause affected another cause, which may have led to something else happening.

Effects of the Flood:

Having explained how the flood was caused you now need to cover the reasons that it had such a big effect in Bangladesh by looking at the effects that it had. You will need to look at things like disease, health and homelessness as well as a range of other effects. You need to think carefully about how the fact that Bangladesh is a poorer nation changes the effect that the flood had.

Conclusion:

In your final section you need to draw together all of your ideas to answer the question at the top of the page and explain your findings. You will have to try and consider how the fact that Bangladesh is a poorer nation changes the effect that the flood had.

Word bank:

Access	Family	Links with	Savings
Bare	Food	Livelihood	Sewage
Because	Health	Malaria	Snow
Deforestation	Homeless	Poverty	Soil
Delta	Housing	Risk	Water
Diarrhoea	Income	Resources	Which meant
Disease	Level of development	Run-off	Work

Why did the flood of 1998 have such a big effect in Bangladesh?

Task:

Your task is to produce a photostory which answers the above question using the photographs that you have been given. You will use the photos as the different screenshots, and will then write the words that the narrator would say over over the top to tell the story.

You will need to give some background as to where Bangladesh is, and to explain what the causes and effects of the flooding were. After that you must then answer the above questions using all the information at your fingertips to come to your own conclusion. You must use at least five of the photographs to tell your story, and must think carefully about what is in your picture and what you are writing for the narrator to say.

Writing Frame:

Introduction:
Bangladesh is located …
The landscape of Bangladesh is …
In 1998 Bangladesh …

Causes of the Flood:
One cause of the flooding was …
This meant that …
The floods happened …
Dhaka was flooded …
A further cause of the flooding was …

Effects of the Flood:
One effect of the flooding was …
This meant that …
Another effect was …
This meant that …
Another group of people affected by the flood were …
Some people were affected more than others …

Conclusion:
So in conclusion, the floods of 1998 had a big effect in Bangladesh because …
This happened because …

Word bank:

Bare	Food	Savings
Because	Health	Sewage
Deforestation	Homeless	Soil
Delta	Housing	Water
Diarrhoea	Livelihood	Which meant
Disease	Poverty	Work
Family	Run-off	

Thinking for Learning

Planning for transfer: making choices (decision-making)

Larkman First School

Despite knowing that their children were learning, Larkman First School in Norfolk wanted to understand why the pupils were not using what they were taught in other contexts. After looking carefully at particular lessons, including one in which it was hoped that the children would use their mathematical skills in answering questions in science relating to plant growth, the school decided that it needed to amend its teaching strategies. They had concluded that it was not the pupils' inability to transfer, but that they had not made the connection; the pupils needed to be explicitly taught to transfer and to be given the time and the space to think.

At the end of some Thinking for Learning lessons teachers may ask the explicit question, 'In what other lessons or situations might you use this technique?' Pupils may list these, or keep an on-going log of new strategies as they learn and develop them. This transfer of new skills becomes most successful when pupils can see the relevance and usefulness of them in their own lives: deciding which new pair of trainers to buy, whether it is a good idea to buy a pet, or if is it really worthwhile leaving home to set up in a flat. Below are some examples of this.

Pupils in Year 5/6 were introduced to a passage from *Charlotte's Web* by E. B. White. In this passage (see below) Mr Arable is faced with a dilemma: should he kill the weak piglet, the runt, or should he give in to Fern's pleas for mercy. The pupils' initial response to this question was predictable, but using the 'Choices' template on page 155 they were encouraged to think more analytically by:

1. In pairs/groups brainstorming all the possible solutions to the problem. For example: go ahead and kill the runt, give it to Fern to look after, say you will spare it but kill it later, give it to the local school, kill Fern instead!

2. Choosing one option that appeals to most.

3. Thinking of all the possible positive (Pros) and negative (Cons) consequences of this choice. This is best done in pairs, taking it in turns to deal with one another's choice.

4. Weighing up the Pros and Cons. Thinking about the importance of each of them, not just the number for or against.

5. Making a final choice to go ahead with this option or not.

6. If *not*, choosing another option and repeating.

153

Having used this technique with the given extract, teachers in one school then went on to study the landing of the Pilgrims in America. The Pilgrims came across natives already living on this 'new' land. What should they do? Pupils used the same technique to study this issue, a good example of very 'near' transfer.

Choices: an extract from Charlotte's web by E. B. White[44]

'Where is Papa going with that ax?' said Fern to her mother as they were setting the table for breakfast.

'Out to the hoghouse,' replied Mrs Arable. 'Some pigs were born last night.'

'I don't see why he needs an ax,' continued Fern, who was only eight.

'Well,' said her mother, 'one of the pigs is a runt. It's very small and weak, and it will never amount to anything. So your father has decided to do away with it.'

'Do away with it?' shrieked Fern. 'You mean kill it? Just because it's smaller than the others?'

Mrs Arable put a pitcher of cream on the table. 'Don't yell, Fern!' she said. 'Your father is right. The pig would probably die anyway.'

Fern pushed a chair out of the way and ran outdoors. The grass was wet and the earth smelled of springtime. Fern's sneakers were sopping by the time she caught up with her father.

'Please don't kill it,' she sobbed. 'It's unfair.'

Mr Arable stopped walking.

'Fern,' he said gently, 'you will have to learn to control yourself.'

'Control myself?' yelled Fern. 'This is a matter of life and death, and you talk about controlling myself.' Tears ran down her cheeks and she took hold of the ax and tried to pull it out of her father's hand.

'Fern,' said Mr Arable, ' I know more about raising a litter of pigs than you do. A weakling makes trouble. Now run along!'

'But it's unfair,' cried Fern. 'The pig couldn't help being born small, could it? If I had been very small at birth, would you have killed me?'

Mr Arable smiled. 'Certainly not,' he said, looking down at his daughter with love. 'But this is different. A little girl is one thing, a runty pig is another.'

'I see no difference,' replied Fern, still hanging onto the ax. 'This is the most terrible case of injustice I have every heard of.'

Extract reproduced by permission of Penguin Books Ltd

Tyne Valley

In a Northumberland High School in the Tyne Valley pupils were introduced to concept maps in geography. They used this technique initially in the study of natural disasters in Year 9. The technique was used again when studying settlement later in the year. Careful planning and liaison allowed science teachers to use the concept mapping technique when studying the rock cycle in Year 10 (Far Transfer).

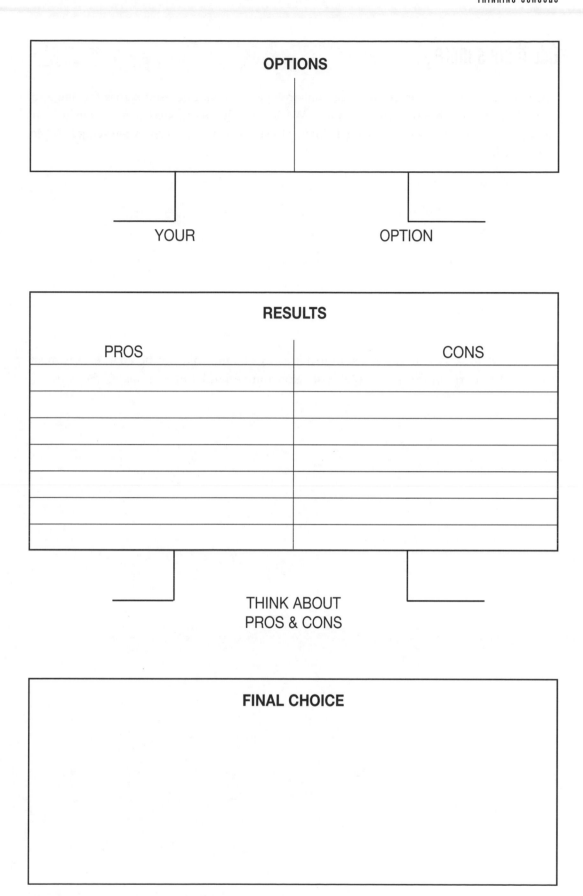

OPTIONS

YOUR   OPTION

RESULTS

PROS	CONS

THINK ABOUT
PROS & CONS

FINAL CHOICE

Choices Template

And there's more . . .

There are a number of practical classroom strategies that can be used across the age and subject range in Thinking for Learning. We have only mentioned a few here in our examples of how to begin applying Thinking for Learning strategies in the school. Some others include:

- ✪ Diamond ranking
- ✪ Fact or Opinion
- ✪ Flowcharts
- ✪ Making Predictions
- ✪ Mind Movies
- ✪ Venn Diagrams.

Practical examples of these for the humanities classroom, that can be adapted for most areas of the curriculum, are available in Northumberland LEA's *Thinking for Learning* file.[15]

156

Review

1 Devise your own Thinking for Learning planning sheet that will allow you to incorporate practically what you have learnt about this approach.

2 What potential benefits do you see in using Philosophy for Children specifically with your pupils?

3 How might 'Reading Photographs' enhance the learning of your class? Select one of the suggested methods, adapt it to use in one of your topics and then find a suitable picture. Reflect on the strategy's success.

4 Select a scheme of work that you have taught before and will be teaching again soon. Try to incorporate thinking strategies across the range of lessons. Reflect on the success of each lesson. Was the children's understanding improved by the use of thinking strategies? Did they enjoy them? How do you think the lessons compared to last year's?

Thinking for learning activity: odd one out

Odd One Out is used to classify and explore relationships between a number of factors. It requires participants to think about the reasons for their choice of the odd one out and can be extended by asking them to make further suggestions for the categories they have put forward, as seen on page 124.

Which one of these activities is the odd one out? Explain why and then ask a colleague for their opinion and explanation. Discuss your responses.

Odd One Out

Concept Maps

Memory Maps

Thinking about change

Preview

The TTA funded North East School-Based Research Consortium: their experiences and recommendations

Developing teachers' practice

Initiating change: where to begin

Utilising action research

This chapter will provide explanations of how to develop a **Thinking for Learning approach**, specifically:

Why ethos is important

Understanding the fluidity and complexity of change

The importance of 'tinkering'

Choosing a 'top-down' or 'bottom-up' approach

The impact on continuing professional development

THINKING ABOUT CHANGE

CHAPTER 5

THEORY

Fullan
- process
  - 'moral purpose'
  - flexible
  - complex
- components
  - knowledge creation
  - collaboration

Hargreaves
- learning schools

PRACTICE

NESBRC
- two examples
  - Head's perspective
  - recommendations
- 'top-down'
- 'bottom-up'
- ethos

PROFESSIONAL DEVELOPMENT
- action research
- networks
- R & D
- M.Ed
- BPRS
- coaching

◆ Time to change

Whether you are deemed a 'successful' school with excellent results, or labelled as 'failing', there is little quantifiable evidence to show whether your leavers have been prepared adequately for what lies in later life. We began this book by discussing the idea of a 'useful' education, one that goes beyond SAT and GCSE results. What we have been proposing should not only maintain or improve your academic grades, but should develop the individual's abilities to cope with future learning and the post-school world that they face. We hope that these learners will have become more 'rounded' because of the self-esteem and confidence that has been built up in their schools by Thinking for Learning.

So this chapter deals with change. It discusses some ideas about change and how to approach it. Brief examples are provided from across the country, but the main focus is on how one group of Northumberland schools went about adopting a Thinking for Learning approach. We hope that this overview of experiences will provide the motivation and ideas for how your school could best implement change. We believe it is a process worth thinking carefully about.

Thinking for Learning nationwide

In Norfolk, the *Thinking Schools: Thinking Children* project was launched in autumn 2000 with a headteachers' conference looking at Accelerated Learning. Since then, the primary phase schools have been developing the use of Visual, Auditory and Kinesthetic learning styles in the classroom, looking at the importance of Emotional Intelligence and at the use of Circle Time and Thinking Strategies. Esteemed professionals in these fields have been involved, such as Robert Fisher, Karin Murris, John Abbott, Oliver Caviglioli and Vivienne Baumfield who focused on the work in the North East of England on investigating teaching thinking in the classroom. But most important has been the involvement and enthusiasm of the teachers in researching and trying out the practical applications in these areas. Many have become involved through action research with Best Practice Research Scholarships, and the education advisory service now produces a newsletter to spread the good practice and experiences of those involved throughout the county.

See Appendices **D** and **E** for two examples of Norfolk BPRSs

Change, innovation and chaos

> Change is complex. The link between cause and effect is difficult to trace, change unfolds in non-linear ways, paradoxes and contradictions abound and creative solutions arise out of interaction under conditions of uncertainty, diversity and instability.
>
> *Michael Fullan*[45]

We find Michael Fullan's work both challenging and reassuring. He seems to be saying that no one can tell you precisely how to change your organisation into the one you think you want. Even knowing where you would like to be after a certain period of time is problematic because A does not necessarily move on to B and then C. At each juncture there can be several resulting spin-offs. Following any one of these will lead to more, probably *ad infinitum*. Change is extremely complex.

Fullan's quote is based upon the science of Complexity (or Chaos) Theory. So many forces interact that we can never be sure how our plans will turn out. But Fullan does have some guiding principles, or lessons, for us to apply. And these have been gleaned from his many years of practical work in running and studying school districts in North America.

Complex Change Lessons (after Fullan):

1. Moral purpose is complex and problematic.
2. Theories of change and theories of education need each other.
3. Conflict and diversity are our friends.
4. Understand the meaning of operating on the edge of chaos.
5. Emotional Intelligence is anxiety provoking and anxiety containing.
6. Collaborative cultures are anxiety provoking and anxiety containing.
7. Attack incoherence: connectedness and knowledge creation are critical.
8. There is no single solution: craft your own theories and actions by being a critical consumer.

A full reading of Michael Fullan's work is recommended but to us there are some clear messages here:

- **You need a vision to emerge but this comes later. The starting point for change is a 'moral purpose' – we need to know why we want the change and this must be based on the needs of our students.**
- **Change is too complex for us to be able to plan every step along the way. We need to set out on the journey and adapt as we learn.**

✄ Change is both stressful and rewarding – and the balance will be constantly changing as the 'edge of chaos' approaches or recedes.

✄ Collaboration and knowledge creation are key components of change.

The first of these messages might seem alien to some school planners, as often we begin with a vision, which is then planned for at every step. We need to look to the second message for the alternative. That is, be flexible. The 'moral purpose', based on the needs of our students, need not only apply to examination success either. The Berwick RAIS Project, for example, cites some traditional educational objectives as purposes, but also refers to 'raised aspirations' and 'healthier lifestyles' as key outcomes they hope to achieve.[46]

So, are you ready to embrace change? Are you a learning school?

Thinking for Learning nationwide

Like Thinking for Learning, *Mind Friendly Learning* in Cheshire emphasises the importance of process in teaching and learning. Led by Peter Greenhalgh, Senior Adviser for Special Education (Inclusion), the project took forward the Director's intention to give equal priority to raising educational standards and to nurturing genuine learning in its broadest sense. It was about empowering all learners to take more control of their learning, expanding and enhancing the capacity to learn, so as to enable the individual to survive and thrive throughout life. The programme drew upon current research and best practice about learning, encompassing Thinking Skills, Accelerated Learning, aspects of Neuro-Linguistic Programming and Emotional Intelligence.

The initiative had a number of key elements:

* An INSET programme to introduce the 'Mind Friendly Learning Framework'.

* A web site development that would offer research, planning aids, tool kits and a portal to other web sites for teachers.

* The establishment of a 'Mind Friendly' Training Team comprising of teachers, advisers and learning support personnel.

* The development of a set of Learner Entitlements.

* Networked training and dissemination across the Advisory Service and the Learning Support Service to ensure that the work was embedded in the national strategies, e.g. Literacy, Numeracy and KS3, and within the subject advisers' INSET and support to schools.

* A celebratory two-day event attended by more than 700 Cheshire headteachers, teachers, learning support assistants and governors.

Mind Friendly Learning is now an embedded aspect of the work of the Advisory Service and the Learning Support Service and many Cheshire schools.

◆ Learning schools

If the Complex Change Lessons do not seem too daunting, then your school probably already meets most of the following, which are set out by David Hargreaves as the characteristics of a Learning School. If you relish the idea of challenge and change, then it would be unsurprising to find that many of these apply to your school.

★ Professional talk and interdependence

★ Action learning (action research) amongst teachers

★ Deprivatisation of teaching and transparency

★ Mentoring and coaching amongst teachers

★ External networking

★ Distributed leadership

★ High expectations

★ Innovation and risk taking

★ 'Tinkering' time.

The last point is an appealing notion: the idea of teachers being encouraged to adapt their teaching methods as they develop or encounter new ideas by 'tinkering'. As reflective practitioners, we would argue that this is something that comes naturally to many of us. However, sometimes our planning needs to be rather more radically altered than this might suggest, but often a little bit of tinkering has profound effects. An example of this occurred quite recently.

Dougal's lesson

Dougal is a very competent secondary school teacher. He was teaching a Year 8 class and they were explaining the causes of World War I, largely as a review activity. The lesson was satisfactory but the students were very passive and by the end of the lesson it was not that clear whether many of them had learned much. The lesson went like this:

1 A brief reminder from the teacher about the topic.

2 A lengthy exposition from the teacher about nine causes of the war as outlined on a worksheet. There was some teacher/pupil interaction here, but responses from the pupils were very brief. This went on for about 20 minutes. (In this time many had contributed nothing to the lesson.)

3 The pupils were then asked to rank order the nine causes of WWI by discussing them (in pairs) and allocating a rank to each one (15 minutes). Most of them stayed on task and tried to complete the exercise but found it quite demanding. Interest levels were moderate.

4 The teacher asked for feedback from the pairs and got a little, but at a fairly low level. He then summarised for the pupils what he thought they had learnt.

When we discussed this lesson later, we agreed that the pupils had not been involved enough. So Dougal did a little tinkering with planning the same lesson for a second Year 8 group. This time:

1 After a very brief welcome/introduction pairs of pupils were given the same worksheet but asked to cut out the nine statements and arrange them in rank order using the 'Diamond-Ranking' technique (see page 99). If they needed clarification about the statements, they could ask; interestingly very few needed to even though Dougal had spent 20 minutes doing this in the previous lesson.

2 Whilst the pupils completed this task – and all were on-task and interested, with a lot of quite heated discussion about where each belonged – Dougal was able to circulate, clarify points where necessary, eavesdrop for interesting comments and perceptions, and intervene to move discussions on.

3 After a very busy 20 minutes one pair was asked to present their rank order. The rest of the class was asked to listen carefully and to explain where their ranking was different and why. This led to a great deal of difference of opinion, some argument (some need for working on the conventions of class discussion) and a much greater depth of understanding than was evident in the previous group.

4 After 15 minutes of this discussion the pairs were asked to revisit their ranking, change it if they felt it was now appropriate and write a brief justification for the 'top' and 'bottom' ranks. (This was followed up in more detail in a later lesson.)

5 The last ten minutes of the lesson were spent reviewing the activity, in terms of both content and method. The pupils had clearly valued the chance to work collaboratively, to listen to others' points of view and to be able to change their responses. It began to emerge that they were beginning to understand the difference between short-term ('trigger') causes and longer-term ('background') causes of such large-scale political events. There was not time to get into this in detail but the previous class had shown none of this level of understanding. It would also have been useful, perhaps in a later lesson, to have discussed how trigger and background factors might apply to events in their own lives – like falling out with friends or parents.

All in all a successful bit of tinkering that required very little change in terms of planning. As David Hargreaves says, tinkering gets even better when we share it, so we need:

★ Individual tinkering

★ Team tinkering

★ Shared tinkering

★ Tinkering observed.

165

Thinking for Learning nationwide

A self-managing team at Paulsgrove Primary School in Portsmouth is looking at the potential of *Thinking Classrooms*. At the end of the year the feasibility of introducing these across the school will be discussed with the staff. The Thinking Classroom is one that utilises Thinking Skills strategies and Accelerated Learning techniques within the supportive learning environment, something we have come to know as Thinking for Learning.

In their work, Mike Fleetham and the rest of the team have been developing this approach for the school since September 2001. On Wednesdays they meet to discuss the work done since the last meeting and where they should concentrate their efforts in the forthcoming week. Mike then informs a six-pupil council in his class of what was decided and this information is passed to the rest of the class during Friday's Circle Time. In this way, not only are the pupils 'dealt in' to their learning, but it is also presented to them by their peers and within the safe and open environment of the circle. It is another way of disseminating the Big Picture.

◆ Top-down or bottom-up?

This idea of tinkering and Fullan's messages about change lead us to a fundamental discussion for the implementation of Thinking for Learning: top-down or bottom-up? It is difficult to label any change as completely one or the other.

Below, we look at the North East School-Based Research Consortium and explore how Thinking for Learning was introduced into those schools. But first we would like to look at an example of implementation that was predominantly bottom-up, which helps demonstrate the diversity of approach when it comes to applying Thinking for Learning in individual schools.

Allendale First School

Lynn Johnston, a classroom teacher at Allendale, first became interested in Thinking Skills when she completed a module on it at the University of Newcastle during her MEd. Although the Head at the time was not enthusiastic about taking the school in this direction, the Deputy was, but left soon after for his own headship. The more she looked into it, the more interested Lynn became. With the arrival of a new Head at the school, who was happy to allow her to pursue Thinking Skills, she was provided with funding to complete a course on it and to buy the Top Ten Thinking Tactics.

The Head had been keen on trying a 'bolt-on' version, possibly in order to minimise the amount of disruption caused across the school, but became increasingly interested in it himself as it appeared to make the children more thoughtful. It seemed to have a particularly profound effect on the confidence of some children with special educational needs.

Staff began to observe Lynn and, by the second year of this initiative, had begun introducing the course into their classrooms. They found that the structured activities gave them support and provided enough knowledge of each 'tactic' for them to use the plans with confidence.

Since then, other thinking activities have been introduced by the staff and the development of a Thinking for Learning approach has been written into the action plan for 2001/02 (see Appendix B2). This includes P4C being investigated, all teachers taking Level 1 of the Thinking Skills Teaching Certificate (see 181) and cross-phase development being discussed with the middle and high schools.

In three years, Allendale First is firmly on board with Thinking for Learning – and all from the interest and persistence of one of the classroom teachers! This is a poignant example of how Thinking for Learning can be implemented through a bottom-up approach, albeit with the support of the Head. A 'bolt-on' strategy in a single classroom has grown to encompass the whole school and beyond (though the other schools were running their own initiatives). The vision is to provide a co-ordinated approach to the development of Thinking for Learning from Reception through to Year 13.

◆ The North East School-Based Research Consortium (NESBRC)

In 1998 a group of schools together with three LEAs and Newcastle University responded to a proposal from the TTA to sponsor a school-based research network that would support professional development through enabling teachers to engage in and with research and produce evidence to help develop teaching and learning in this country. As the research would be classroom based, it was obviously hoped that disseminating this new knowledge would encourage other teachers to see the relevance of it to them and their own classrooms. The outcomes would produce teachers enhancing their own professional development, whilst sharing good practice and leading to improving standards nationwide.

The University of Newcastle saw an opportunity to develop what had already begun in recent years. There was a history of collaboration in the north east with Thinking Skills as the focus: the university's MEd provides two modules on Thinking Skills with the emphasis on action research and coaching; PGCE tutors sent forth legions of PGCE students into the schools, providing another entry for Thinking Skills; and Northumberland LEA had been encouraging investigation and dissemination into the area for several years. With all this focus, it was decided that the bid for the TTA funding

167

would be to investigate the efficacy and application of Thinking Skills in the classroom. The LEAs of Northumberland, Newcastle and North Tyneside and six high schools, Prudhoe, Heaton Manor, Walker, Kenton, Longbenton and latterly St Benet Biscop, were all keen to participate and the bid went ahead. They were successful.

We have tried to map out the development of Thinking for Learning in the north east on the opposite page, finishing at the most recent stage, the North East School-Based Research Consortium.

The TTA funding expired in 2001, but the consortium is looking at moving its work forward further. One way currently being investigated is through applying for funding to establish network learning communities. As the consortium has already produced some excellent work with the TTA's help, it is hoped that they will be able to continue to produce and disseminate the new knowledge that has been created within their own classrooms with the help and expertise from their LEAs and the university.

Case studies

Below are examples from two of the schools involved in the NESBRC's work. We hope that these will provide a useful overview of how change has occurred and some of the outcomes that have arisen from their involvement in the consortium. We have also summarised the thoughts of a headteacher involved in the project and provided a list of recommendations from what has been learnt in these last three years. We would like to thank the schools involved, Vivienne Baumfield from the University of Newcastle and the TTA for allowing us to use this information.

St Benet Biscop RC High School, Bedlington
Context

St Benet Biscop is the only Catholic High School in Northumberland, but also draws on up to 11 non-Catholic Middle Schools. Its intake spans the whole ability range, with 62 pupils on the special educational needs register, 21 of these have statements. The school currently has 881 on the roll (213 in the sixth form) and is oversubscribed.

There are plans for further improvements in facilities at the school. A new centre is intended for the increasingly popular sixth form and the community will soon have access to media, music and drama facilities. The school is also a provider of training in installing and maintaining computer networks.

St Benet Biscop was already a reasonably successful school when it was inspected by OFSTED in 1997. But the school was not satisfied with what it heard from the inspectors. It felt that it was reaching the end of a period of development. The new Head and his senior colleagues realised that something needed to be done if decline and demoralisation were not to set in. And they recognised that 'Learning' was at the heart of it.

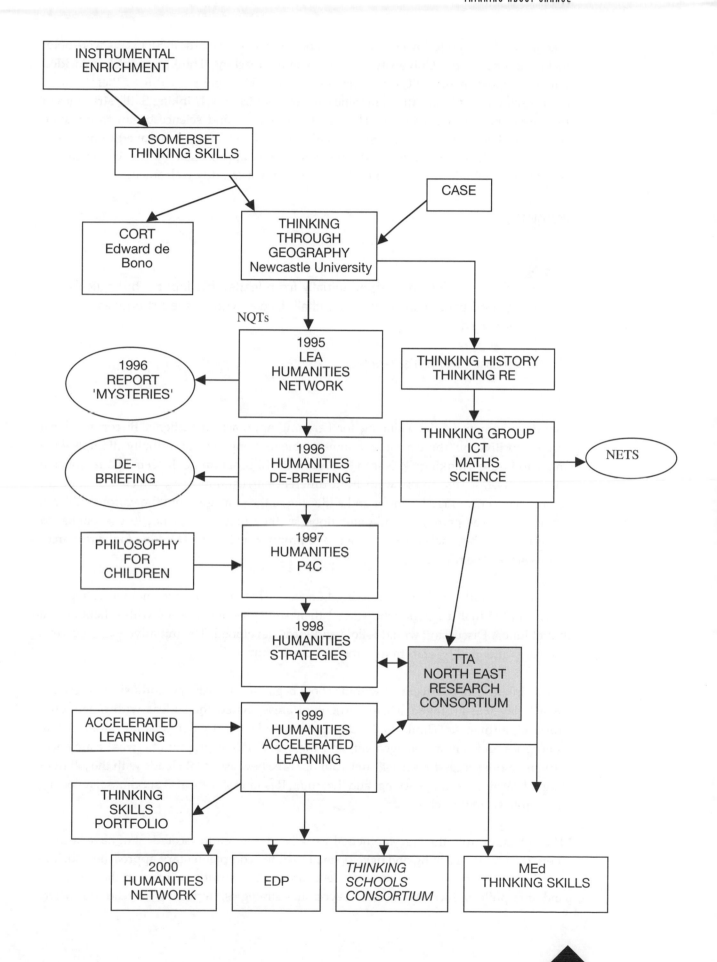

Meetings of key staff followed, focusing on how to move forward. INSET days were held, including one by the University of Newcastle on Teaching Thinking, which coincided with the appointment of NQTs who had experienced Thinking Skills during their training at the university. Initially, the humanities department trialled Thinking Skills strategies in the classroom – using Thinking Through Geography – and science began to integrate some into their teaching, but cross-curricular groups were also encouraged to meet and discuss the ideas. Soon afterwards, the school was approached by the University of Newcastle to join the TTA-funded NESBRC, which was readily welcomed.

Development

Thinking skills developed initially from leadership input – but quickly gained pace from staff at the chalk face – who pushed the ideas forward.

NESBRC Co-ordinator, St Benet Biscop

The development of the Thinking for Learning approach at St Benet Biscop has been largely positive, but there have been some problems along the way. Initially attempts were made to infuse Thinking Skills into the Year 9 PSHE programme. It seemed a reasonable place to start, as the tutors were from different curriculum areas, which was thought should have encouraged transfer and a filtering of the strategies into the various subjects. However, it was perhaps a little ambitious, as they had decided not to use published materials and they lacked the experience to produce their own Thinking Skills resources at this stage. The trial failed.

Undeterred, staff developed 'Thinking Lunches'. This optional, informal workshop was led by individual teachers, who shared their strategies and lessons with others over a buffet lunch. Discussion would follow and ideas developed. The initiative was a success, regularly attended by staff from across the curriculum.

The Thinking Skills movement within school began to flourish and enthusiasm grew. An INSET day was arranged where curriculum areas shared their ideas with others on a carousel format; a 'Think Tank' day encouraged staff to demonstrate strategies to colleagues and senior management; and the Year 9 PSHE programme was relaunched, proving more successful second time round. Three new assistant Heads with the job titles 'Pupil Learning', 'Staff Learning' and 'Learning Resources' were also appointed, reflecting the emphasis in the school.

The outcomes from this developmental work have been multi-faceted. Staff have become more focused on learning and have opened to other, complementary approaches, such as Accelerated Learning. They have been encouraged to try out new ideas in the classroom and are philosophical about less successful strategies, reflecting instead on where improvements could be made. Interest in what they are involved in was indicated in threshold applications: 24 out of 32 mentioned Thinking Skills as an area of strength and development.

The focusing of minds on learning has had other benefits too. Teachers have become aware of the implications of involvement in these initiatives on their professional development. They feel part of a wider learning community, with staff being asked to present at conferences, being invited to the United States on the Teachers' International Professional Development programme and taking part in international research. In these ways they share and develop their expertise, the beneficiaries of which include the increasing number of ITT students who are being mentored in the school by numerous staff.

The work continues. Thinking Skills and Accelerated Learning have become common components of lessons in most subjects. Strategies are continually being updated, not least through new staff bringing in ideas to curriculum areas. Eight teachers are undertaking research projects and colleagues eagerly replicate or practise different strategies across the curriculum. The school also views the links with the University of Newcastle as a vital source of expertise and guidance.

After a number of years of development, awareness raising and some false starts the focus, maintained by the Head, has always been on learning. He was able to take those feelings of knowing something must happen to encourage further improvement and use them to motivate the staff into creating a Thinking for Learning environment. This was truly a top-down approach, constantly motivated and maintained by him and his management team.

Go to Appendix F for examples of some of the developments within the subject areas

- ✪ Whole school awareness raising. Staff Training Day with Alistair Smith (Accelerated Learning).

- ✪ Contact with University of Newcastle Thinking Through Geography (David Leat).

- ✪ Membership of North East School-Based Research Consortium (Thinking Skills), funded by TTA Partnership with six schools, three LEAs and University of Newcastle.

- ✪ Departmental bid for funds to develop Thinking Skills. £1,500 for 1999–2000. Funding for supply cover to enable pairs of staff to plan a TS lesson, observe each other and discuss evaluations. Six staff at two days each = £1,200.

- ✪ Consultancy from University and LEA. Networking with LEA humanities group and University geography group.

- ✪ Dissemination to rest of staff. Thinking Skills handbook prepared.

- ✪ Development of role of 'Teacher Coach' to work with colleagues across departments (ongoing).

- ✪ Wider dissemination via Regional Dissemination Conferences, LEA Portfolio, National Conferences.

✪ Best Practice Research Scholarships to continue work and research into impact.

✪ 'Thinking Lunches'. School supplies lunch for colleagues to meet monthly and discuss good practice: 15 to 20 attend, all departments.

✪ International study visit to USA – April 2001.

Prudhoe Community High School

Context

Situated within the town of Prudhoe, the school has a varied intake across the ability range. It is well thought of locally and currently has over 960 on roll, including a large sixth form. The school became a Technology College in summer 1995 and was awarded Beacon status in spring 1999. Despite its size, there is a warm family ethos to the school.

Proud of its relationship with the feeder schools at all levels, Prudhoe has worked well with them over a number of years. Together they were successful in obtaining over £2 million of funding for educational aspects of a Single Regeneration Bid. The bid included a Thinking Skills strand. They also have strong links with industry and are currently expanding pre- and post-16 vocational courses with the help of local employers.

Prior to the formation of the NESBRC, Prudhoe and its feeder schools have been working closely with Northumberland LEA and the University of Newcastle to develop Thinking Skills. CASE was being used in the science department and, together with the Middle Schools and funding from the Technology College bid, an examination of CAME was underway. During the consortium's existence, Prudhoe has also used funding from its Beacon status to work with its feeder schools to develop Thinking for Learning.

There was already a strong link between the humanities department and PGCE tutors at the university. This proved key in involving the school in the NESBRC.

Development

In school, the NESBRC was first viewed almost as a humanities initiative, partly because much of the work seemed driven by that department and that the benefits to the rest of the school remained unclear. There had also been changes in the senior management team, including a new Head and four different school co-ordinators for the project. Communication needed work to raise the profile of the NESBRC within the school.

The breakthrough came with the humanities department's involvement with interested feeder schools. They had been looking at infusing Thinking Skills into the curriculum and led workshops about them, raising their status. Further progress was made when the First Schools who had been working with the university prompted a debate into the mutual benefits of the different initiatives. Cross-phase workshops were introduced, which engaged staff and promoted the wider issues of teaching and learning as well as the positive effect on the professional development of staff. The initiatives were written into a coherent school development policy, pulling the staff together behind it and focusing many on the advantages for all of Thinking for Learning.

As their work progresses, they have recognised the need for more time to generate ideas and for clearer communication, especially for disseminating these ideas. Of particular importance to the school has been the access they have had to the expertise at the university.

A headteacher's perspective

From a head's point of view, there have been a number of issues about what involvement in the NESBRC has meant to the school and its staff. These are summarised below.

- School co-ordinator: the lynchpin in maintaining the consortium focus and in ensuring that the school keeps to what it has agreed

- Senior management team: vital to provide the encouragement and resources for staff to share and develop their ideas. Important not to set any specific targets or expectations at the beginning, but to support the ideas as they emerge.

- Heads of department: important for maintaining commitment, but do not need to be actively involved in the projects.

- Teachers: take an idea and try it out for themselves. They then bring in more colleagues, who like what they see and develop it in their own classrooms.

- Development: resist any tendency for cliques by using cross-curricular development wherever possible. Involvement in the consortium has broken down isolation by promoting team teaching and learning from each other. Support efficient networking across the consortium and other schools. Subject networks across schools focusing on Thinking Skills can often be a key to enthusing new members of staff.

Impact of the NESBRC:

- Shift in focus from teaching to how pupils' learn. This can be seen in an improvement in the quality of lessons and in the discussions amongst staff.

- Awareness of potential of Thinking Skills to subject development.

- Helped create the right climate in school for Continuing Professional Development (CPD) by creating a collaborative and co-operative ethos.

- CPD seen as central to the raising of pupil attainment. The enthusiasm and enjoyment of teaching and learning in the school that has been generated must have a positive impact on pupils.

- Sharing expertise at seminars and conferences and writing for professional journals has had a positive effect on staff.

- Funding had an important role to play in supporting the development of new approaches to CPD, including creative approaches to timetabling.

⊠ Mentoring of ITT students has been an important aspect of involvement in the consortium as it promoted reflection on teaching and learning, created a need to develop a common vocabulary and an interest in improving classroom practice for the mentor.

⊠ Understanding of pupil learning and Thinking Skills deemed important in the recruitment of new staff, particularly heads of department.

We are not looking for short-term or easily measured indicators but for the development in the long term of a culture of learning in the school.

Recommendations arising from the work of the NESBRC

Drawing upon the experience of the North East School-Based Research Consortium, we have identified a number of factors that schools contemplating becoming involved in any similar initiatives should consider.

Planning

☆ Establish common goals and clear objectives with all the partners. Agree commitments, time scales and outcomes.

☆ Incorporate meetings and cross-consortium commitments into the school calendar to ensure dates are set in the calendars of all the schools involved.

☆ Encourage all members to contribute a financial stake to ensure commitment and create expectations of the consortium.

☆ Allow for initial flexibility before identifying where support and structure will be most needed.

☆ Formalise the school's commitment in the School Development Plan, earmarking resources and identifying desired outcomes.

Internal support

✫ The commitment and enthusiasm of the senior management team in the school is vital.

✫ Aim to create a thinking school, but accept that this is not always possible.

✫ Identify where development can best fit with the needs of teachers. Chalk-face initiatives within a supportive structure will encourage a consortium's success.

✫ Encourage teachers to engage in critical reflection and contribute to the creation of knowledge about learning within a blame-free environment.

External support

* Funding for such initiatives is often available from agencies like the DfES (Best Practice Research Scholarship grants for action research).

* Procuring the support of a higher education institution can be invaluable for the expertise and the learning resources they can often provide.

* Higher education and LEA partners can facilitate integration and help retain a clear focus within and across schools.

* Obtaining exemplar materials and enlisting the help of teachers experienced in Thinking Skills should assist the introduction of these initiatives within a consortium.

The school co-ordinator

* Ensure that they have opportunities to meet and share ideas, as they are pivotal in the development of a consortium and in the dissemination of good practice.

* Create a senior management role for the co-ordinator, as they need to have sufficient authority to effect change. Linking the co-ordinator's role to teaching and learning, staff development or ITT can help achieve synergy.

* Allow the co-ordinator the flexibility to develop a research and evidence informed culture.

* Set aside funding to give the co-ordinator enough time to make the project work.

Research

* Encourage involvement in research (and learning from research).

* Urge the focus to be on the fundamental aspects of learning, rather than just looking at a range of strategies.

* Develop valid and reliable criteria for tracking progress; a combination of quantitative and qualitative methods should be used wherever possible.

* Support methods that will provide coherence between the individual research projects within the school and across the consortium.

* Introduce a mechanism for inducting new staff into the research culture of the school.

* Consider encouraging teachers to be involved in research by paying registration fees for higher degrees from the school budget.

Continuing professional development

✳ Allow different approaches to professional development (e.g. academic, action research, etc.) and opportunities.

✳ Promote reflective practice by encouraging writing at all stages of the individual's study/research to help make sense of it.

✳ Consider working through consortium networks that are role specific (e.g. Newly Qualified Teachers, Heads of Department, etc.), as well as through the usual subject routes.

Dissemination

✰ Encourage individuals to write articles, present papers and lead workshops. Articulating experience in different ways helps develop understanding.

✰ Use the HE institution and LEAs to help establish good national links to broadcast what you are doing to a wider audience.

Six steps for knowledge creation in schools

David Hargreaves suggests that knowledge creation in schools, the way forward for change, could be managed in the following way. We have tried to illustrate below his six steps to how the Thinking for Learning initiative has developed in north east schools.

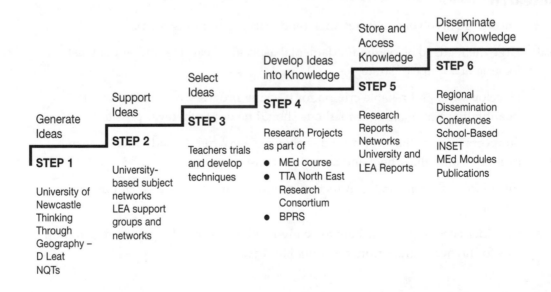

Of course the process is not as linear or straightforward as this. As Michael Fullan suggests, change is a complex phenomenon. Sometimes steps are missed out or are difficult to separate. Dissemination of ideas often takes place before they have been refined or proven into new knowledge. As this book is written, we are trying to consolidate the emerging knowledge about the efficiency of Thinking for Learning in our schools. We are in the process of developing a Teaching Thinking and an Accelerated Learning Certificate to provide a vehicle for dissemination that also recognises teachers' investment in developing new skills.

What is important is that we should never sit back and allow ourselves to believe that we have finally arrived; there will always be room for improvement, but we should still appreciate the progress made. The experience of the NESBRC has been extremely fruitful, but they are still looking to continue their work further. We hope that their experience to date has provided ideas and possibly a template for how Thinking for Learning might be investigated in your school.

◆ Ethos setting

The difference between the example of bottom-up implementation and those of top-down could not have been much more diverse. Whereas one was more tentative and isolated, the other examples showed a flood of activity and initiatives; one involved concerted investment, the other a more low profile approach. There is a considerable difference between the size of the schools, and probably several other variables as well, but this relates to one of the points we wish to raise. With all schools being different, even in the subtlest of ways, no one method of implementation will suit all. What we recommend is that the different possibilities in this chapter be examined and the best one for your school piloted, with any relevant amendments. Flexibility is key, Fullan argues; begin with the moral purpose and adapt the planning as you learn. That may appear equivocal, but it is sound advice.

Whichever way the implementation flows, the right ethos must be a starting point. If heads are not leading the change, then they must be more than open to it: they must be positive about any staff initiative. Ruth Bradley, Head of Allendale Middle School, agreed that ethos was key. When she became head in 1997, her attitude was (and still is) that staff should be the best they can be. With a background in Thinking Skills, she encouraged them through a number of initiatives, as they trialled, then infused, Thinking for Learning strategies. The approach might be considered as one of bottom-up, but she created the ethos for change. The effects on the school have not only been in academic improvement (Key Stage 2 SATs: 61–63 per cent level 4 and above in 1997 to 100 per cent in science in 2000 and 95 per cent in 2001), but also in less tangible ways. For example, the percentage of pupils in the school who play a musical instrument has risen from approximately 9 per cent to 40 per cent. Although a number of factors may account for this, Ruth attributes it to Thinking for Learning and the attitude it has instilled. Certainly, when we visited the school, the atmosphere was one of happy and motivated children.

Another example of change

Sue Joyner and Jay Thacker brought about change at Byrness First School, Northumberland, through using the ALPS[35] approach as a framework. Their focus was humanities (supported by Northumberland's 'Thinking through Humanities' network) and a whole school initiative for behaviour. They saw the onset of Curriculum 2000 as an opportunity to introduce the change.

Their amalgamation of Accelerated Learning and Thinking Skills strategies is a good example of how Thinking for Learning can be practically applied. They did this in two cycles:

CYCLE ONE

Planning	Introduction of an annual audit and action plan on Thinking Skills as part of the School Improvement Plan. Adaptation of our medium-term planning, highlighting opportunities for Visual, Auditory and Kinesthetic strategies (e.g. Kenya plan in geography [Years 2–4] and The Seaside [Early Years and Year 1]). Use of a lesson plan model based on the ALPS approach (e.g. geography lesson plan).
Environment	Change in policy on display – classrooms used as a learning tool (visual cues and keywords) rather than for celebrating pupils' work (that is found in corridors and hall). Classrooms rearranged to reflect learning zones.
Behaviour	Change positive behaviour system to include a 'brainy box' and certificates to be used during celebration assembly. The implementation of a weekly Circle Time.

Go to Appendix C for the Seaside and Kenya schemes of work, as well as the example of a geography lesson

What now?

Thinking for Learning in a school is an exciting prospect. This book has looked at various methods within Thinking for Learning, the evidence for it, in which way the approaches might be implemented and provided some examples of what has been happening around the country. But what next?

CYCLE TWO

Monitoring and Evaluation	Review the teaching and learning policy to reflect ALPS approach and use it as a monitoring tool. Review of the pupils' individual Records of Achievement and target-setting to reflect ALPS strategies.
Specific Strategies	Develop Accelerated Learning classroom strategies: ✴ target cards ✴ marking codes ✴ 'must haves' before showing teacher work ✴ use of music ✴ brain gym ✴ hot seating ✴ thinking-focused plenaries (i.e. metacognitive).

It is too early yet to measure the impact of the Thinking for Learning approach on the pupils' achievement, however, there are some positive indications already. Through classroom observation it has been noted that the children are now more able to express and demonstrate their thinking. Their knowledge of subjects seems to be improving too. As we have been at pains to state throughout this book, highlighting process should not negatively affect the learning of content. If anything, these strategies should help improve content retention. Sue and Jay report that the children were 'unbearably smug' about their understanding and knowledge of the then-history topic when the link inspector visited. They claim he seemed quite overwhelmed!

Both teachers and pupils seem to enjoy learning this way. The older children show signs of becoming more critical thinkers, 'not satisfied with one simple answer'.

Behaviour and attitudes to learning have improved throughout the school as a result of adopting a Thinking for Learning approach. The success of the work being done at Byrness First School was also reflected in many of the positive comments made in a recent OFSTED inspection.

◆ Developing teaching practice

In a speech given at the Institute of Education soon after becoming chief executive of the QCA, David Hargreaves argued strongly that the new economy of the twenty-first century requires workers with problem-solving and interpersonal skills. Whilst traditional teaching methods may have their place in establishing basic skills and knowledge, the development of these more sophisticated 'Thinking Skills' requires a different approach. Those in the best position to develop these new approaches are teachers, working with support from educational researchers in higher education and others.

'If teachers are not involved in innovative activity, they are not likely to understand how to create the conditions in which students learn how to be innovative.'

David Hargreaves [47]

David Hargreaves has previously spoken about the need for students to acquire the skills they will need for the 'Knowledge Age' that we are now entering, where economic success requires the ability to constantly generate, and implement, new forms of knowledge. Teachers can be involved in knowledge creation through small-scale action research and innovation. Hargreaves has referred to this as 'Tinkering with Practice in the Classroom'.

This process of innovation and small-scale action research is well under way in some of our schools and many teachers are reporting benefits for both themselves and their pupils from this renewed focus on what works best in the classroom. Some examples of how this has been supported within Northumberland are outlined below. Some of these benefits may also be open to your school.

- **Best Practice Research Scholarships**: In the first year of this DfEE(DfES)-funded scheme more than 20 teachers in Northumberland received research grants of up to £3,000 to undertake a piece of small-scale, very focused classroom research. Most of these were looking at the impact of the introduction of Thinking for Learning in the classroom. A second bid for 15 grants was successful in 2001/2 and group bids for 2002/3 have been submitted on behalf of a further 30 teachers in Northumberland, including one group working with the Berwick RAIS project.

- **MEd Thinking Skills' Modules**: The University of Newcastle offers two modules of study on Thinking Skills as part of its MEd programme. Approximately 60 Northumberland teachers have completed Module 1 (taught) and 20 have gone on to study Module 2 (action research). We have been fortunate in being able to offer these MEd modules as 'outposted' courses that are taught during the day. Costs have been subsidised by a TTA grant and by individual teachers using the £500 DfEE Bursary made available as a pilot within a limited number of LEAs.

- **The North East School-Based Research Consortium**: This three-year, TTA-funded research consortium consists of a partnership of six high schools, three LEAs and the University of Newcastle. The project finished in March 2001 with a published report to follow. The main focus of the project was on how the implementation of Thinking Skills strategies promoted teachers' own professional development as well as raising pupil achievement.

- **Research and Development Groups**: At least two high schools have standing R&D groups that control their own delegated budget and have responsibility for seeking out and devising new teaching strategies and evaluating their impact. Some smaller middle and first schools have similar, but less formal, arrangements whereby pairs or small groups of teachers undertake similar work.

- **Thinking Humanities Network**: Since 1995 over 70 teachers have received small grants through the LEA's Standards Fund to attend a series of network sessions, trial and evaluate Thinking Skills strategies.

○ **Northumberland's Teaching Thinking Certificate**: In March 2001 the Northumberland Teaching Thinking Certificate was introduced and 100 teachers had completed Level 1 by the end of 2001. The course consists of four taught sessions with teachers trialling at least three strategies in their classrooms, evaluating their impact and having at least one of these sessions observed.

By seeking out and utilising relatively small amounts of support a large number of teachers have been able to do some very significant 'tinkering' in their own classrooms. The results of this tinkering are being shared through a number of DfES, TTA and LEA publications and many of these teachers contributed excellent workshops at the June 2001 Thinking for Learning Conference in Northumberland.

Between them these have provided opportunities for over 200 teachers to be involved to some degree in action research in the area of Thinking Skills. The results of this research are now coming together and point strongly towards the efficacy of Thinking for Learning for:

- ◊ updating teachers' pedagogic skills and their enthusiasm.

- ◊ motivating and interesting pupils of all ages.

- ◊ raising standards in specific areas such as oracy, questioning and enquiry skills, ability to classify, identify causes and effects and different interpretations.

- ◊ Key Stage 3 and at GCSE where there is evidence of higher standards in both science and geography. (Evidence in other subjects has not been quantified but teachers' judgements about the impact of Thinking for Learning are positive.)

◆ Teachers and Action Research

As if life was not busy enough for teachers, now they are expected to get into research too! Yet dozens of teachers in the north east, and elsewhere, have voluntarily become involved in Action Research as part of their MEd course, with the support of the Humanities Network or in receipt of the DfEE's Best Practice Research Scholarships. They do this because they are interested in developing their own skills and understanding about learning.

So what is Action Research? It is not large-scale research projects conducted by academics who look at the work of other people and draw generalisations about teaching and learning. It is:

- ✳ research by individuals on their own work.

- ✳ carried out by teachers who want to introduce change and to evaluate the impact of this change.

❋ about asking questions and hypothesising – not just about trying to find solutions to existing problems.

❋ systematic and planned.

❋ most successful if it is collaborative, working with like-minded colleagues or with the support of a larger network.

❋ most likely to succeed if supported with the expertise of research assistants and tutors from other agencies, such as university departments of education.

❋ based on the collection of evidence and reflection upon the evidence and the process.

❋ about the critical analysis and systematic questioning of existing practice in order to effect desirable changes in the classroom.

Research methods and guidance

Questionnaires	Finding out about pupils' attitudes and what they find helpful/interesting.
Observation	Keeping a record (notes/video/audio) of what happens.
Peer Observation	A colleague observes and keeps the record for future discussion.
Video	Good for later analysis of pupil and teacher behaviours – a good record.
Teacher/Pupil Logs and Diaries	On-going and regular notes help track the progress of a change and its impact.
Interviews	By the teacher or a colleague. Helps explore how pupils feel about the change.
Assessment Task	Tasks designed to assess specific skills, knowledge and understanding. Can be used before, during and after the change for comparison.
Pupil Work	Evaluating the end product of a lesson/unit of work to assess the impact of the change.

All the above are useful but only a few pieces of Action Research would use all of them. Teachers choose those techniques relevant to their study.

Teacher's Action Research is not intended to be an empirical science that will 'prove' the efficacy of a change in an irrefutable way. It is most important to the individual teacher but will be of interest to other colleagues as an indication of changes that seem to be successful or otherwise.

How one teacher got started

- I identified an area of Thinking Skills that I could develop in my own classroom.

- I looked at how my research interest tied in with the School Development Plan.

- I refined the area of Thinking Skills further through more selective reading.

- I produced a timetable for data collection.

- A first analysis of the data/refining the focus.

- Analysis of my research project.

- The next steps – whole school involvement.

Jacqui Harding (former first school teacher, now an Early Years Advisory Teacher in Suffolk)

◆ Continuing professional development for teachers

When we consider the changes taking place in education today, and add to it the messages of this and many other books, it is clear that teachers need the time, the resources and the opportunities to update their teaching knowledge and skills on a regular basis. We are beginning to see signs that the DfES, TTA and some LEAs are recognising this and starting to consider how best to do it. For example, the DfES is considering the extension of funding for Newly Qualified Teachers into the second and third years of their new careers and we have begun to see grants for Best Practice Research Scholarships (BPRS) and Bursaries for Teachers. We need to ensure that these opportunities are going to have an effect by paying attention to what research tells us about teachers' professional development.

In the 1980s Joyce and Showers[13] undertook extensive research into teacher development and suggested this model:

Type of INSET	Level of impact			
	Awareness	Knowledge	Skill	Application
Presentation/Theory	✔			
Demonstration	✔	✔		
Simulated Practice	✔	✔	✔	
Feedback on Performance	✔	✔	✔	✔
Coaching/Support in Classroom	✔	✔	✔	✔

As the aim of any training for teachers must be that they begin to change their practice, then we can see from this model that INSET for teachers really needs to include elements of *feedback* and *coaching* if it is to be effective. This need not necessarily come from the original INSET provider but could come from colleagues or others.

Our own experience of the development of teachers' expertise in the teaching of Thinking for Learning does not contradict this, but there does seem to be a missing or alternative element in this model – that of *continuity* of support. Whilst we have not always been able to provide feedback and coaching in the classroom for the many teachers who have participated in our networks, what they have had is the opportunity to meet, collaborate and share with colleagues on a regular and on-going basis. Thus they can practise new techniques or strategies in their own classrooms and then share their findings in order to refine further their teaching. Where classroom observation has been possible with these groups there is invariably confirmation of what teachers are telling us about the development of their teaching style and its impact upon the pupils.

Coaching

In recent years David Leat at the University of Newcastle has been concentrating on the development of 'teacher coaches' to develop work on Thinking Skills further. This has been a key strand of the TTA funded North East School-Based Research Consortium. Some key points emerging from this work on coaching are:

1. 'You plan, I teach ➡ I plan, you teach' is an excellent and inclusive model of professional development.

2. Peer coaching teams of two or three colleagues work well.

3. Peer coaching works best when heads and deputies participate in both training and practice.

4. Coaching works best when teachers avoid giving advice but use data to promote discussion.

Into the future

So teacher and academic researcher can go hand in hand to develop what is best for the classrooms of today and tomorrow. Whichever way you choose to implement Thinking for Learning, it is always going to be worthwhile to encourage the classroom practitioner to reflect on their teaching and tinker with the lessons. Education is not about being dogmatic; it is about providing the best learning for our children. We may draw on valid research and make suggestions for your school, but it is only you, at the local level and knowing the school's context, who can decide what to keep in and what to throw out.

As teachers are rightly encouraged to continually seek professional development, so schools need to build upon their own successes. This may mean being open to new ideas put forward by current educational and brain research. We firmly believe that Thinking for Learning encapsulates much of what is best about these discoveries. It is a soundly based, practical and worthwhile approach to improving children's attainment. Not only that, it should help to develop the more flexible and rounded citizens that society is demanding for tomorrow.

Review

1. Fullan suggests we need a 'moral purpose' before embarking on change. What would your school's moral purpose be?

2. What links do you have with Higher Education in your area? Ascertain interest in establishing a Thinking for Learning network with other schools, HE and the LEA. Exploit any links you have with institutions already practising and explore the funding possibilities.

3. How would you gauge the ethos in your school? What initiatives or attitudes would help to improve it?

4. What would be the advantages and disadvantages of you carrying out your own action research? Make a note of these and the areas that you would be interested in studying. How could you overcome the disadvantages in order to continue your professional development?

Thinking for learning activity: flowcharts

Flowcharts are used to change serial information from one format to another. They can be used collaboratively in a Thinking for Learning approach, requiring participants to first understand the data before transferring it.

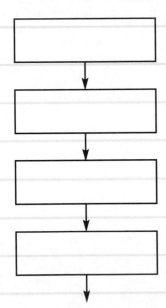

On our path to change it seems sensible that we should adapt as we encounter obstacles, unforeseen challenges or as we learn, yet we should have a basic map before we take the first step.

Using the flowchart format, sketch out a rough map for changing into a Thinking for Learning school.

Appendix A

Tuckswood First School

1 Statement of values

Sue Eagle, Headteacher of Tuckswood First School, came from a background of teaching P4C to young children. When she arrived at the school seven years ago, one of the first things she did was to meet with staff to establish their core beliefs about teaching. From those early discussions arose the school's value statement and from there the practical strategies for improvement.

STATEMENT OF VALUES – TUCKSWOOD FIRST SCHOOL

Our school is committed to promoting a sense of community as well as an individual sense of self-worth.

Our school is to be a community of caring and fairness, of life-long learners, for whom access to knowledge is both a right and a critical achievement.

The following coherent set of values has grown from our learning about the most effective way to achieve our school aims.

The values that the whole staff at Tuckswood County First School base our practice on include the following:

★ Learning for its own sake
★ Developing each person's individual potential
★ Working in a collaborative way
★ Consistent coherence to an agreed set of policies
★ Being learners alongside the children
★ Self-analysis and openness with each other
★ Trust in each other's professional judgements
★ Improvement in quality of our children's experience and attainment.

The values we wish to influence and promote in children's learning include the following:

★ Enthusiasm for learning
★ Persistence in learning
★ Enquiry and curiosity in learning.

The personal values we wish to promote include the following:

★ Openness and optimism in approach
★ Sharing and learning together
★ Self-respect, integrity, honesty and trust
★ Acceptance, courtesy and compassion.

We are committed to the promotion and development of human dignity and human potential.

---

2 Community of learning

Careful use of questioning – paying attention all the time by teachers and classroom assistants to how and why we are questioning – use of open and 'I wonder' questions and encouraging children to hypothesise and discover.

Developing success criteria with the children – 'How will we know if we have been successful?' Returning to the success criteria for review and evaluation session.

Accountability of children for their learning – using thinking time and calling on necessary techniques. Being rigorous when doing this.

Sharing learning success, achievements and 'tussles', e.g. in Sharing Assembly, 'Well Done' tree, etc.

Sharing the learning objectives of activities and tasks at all levels.

Providing opportunities for pupils to be alongside people with a passion about their subject, e.g. visiting poets, etc.

COMMUNITY OF LEARNING

How we work to achieve the aim in our Value Statement:

'Our school is to be a community of caring and fairness, of life-long learners, for whom access to knowledge is both a right and a critical achievement.'

Developing children's involvement in the planning process – 'we need to look at ... what could we do? – what do we want to find out about? ... how can we do this? – Children being historians and investigators.

Context drama work leading from and enhancing story, history, geography, science and RE, AT1 science and maths. Encouraging an investigative empathetic approach.

Careful and consistent teaching of skills across the subject. Assess – plan – teach – assess ...

Brain Gym sessions enabling children to use their whole brain to access and consolidate learning. Open access to water to maximise brain function. Use of variety of music to aid learning.

Teaching skills of mind mapping to help children to follow patterns of thought and think logically and creatively.

Philosophy and Thinking Skills sessions. These are very structured and link with accountability of children for their own learning.

3 Citizenship

Close attention to questioning strategies has been one of the central considerations in the school's improvement. Below are questions used at Tuckswood for citizenship work.

Some useful general questions for citizenship work

- To direct pupils thinking towards a specific issue
  e.g. What do you think about ...?

- To follow the concerns of the pupils
  e.g. Is there anything in the story that you would like to talk about?

- To discover pupils' perception
  e.g. What do you think of that?

- To assess pupils' understanding of a word or concept
  e.g. What do you think that means?

- To encourage pupils to examine or justify an opinion
  e.g. Why do you think that?

- To clarify statement
  e.g. What do you mean by that?

- To assess whether there is a consensus
  e.g. Who agrees with this?

- To encourage pupils to make judgements
  e.g. Do you think that's fair?

- To encourage pupils to predict
  e.g. What do you think will happen next?

- To develop imagination
  e.g. What would you do if ...

- To encourage negotiation
  e.g. Can you agree on ... (e.g. what choice of action is best)?

- To recap or sum up
  e.g. What have we thought about so far?

There has been much progress over the last seven years, which, in the spirit of disseminating good practice, Sue shares at conference seminars and with visitors to the school. We recommend a visit to their website, the address for which can be found at the end of the book.

Allendale First School

1 Thinking skills lesson plan

Allendale First School
Lesson Plan

Date: 14.1.01

Time: 2.00–2.45

Number on roll: 26

Teacher: Lynn Johnston

Subject: History

Number present: 24

Learning Objectives
1   To be able to describe the characteristics of old and new toys.
2   To be able to sequence a variety of toys onto a timeline.

Activity
In this activity the learning objectives will not be discussed with the children before we begin. The idea is that they work out the activity – it makes them think/reason about what they have to do instead to being told.

1   Children given envelopes with pictures of toy and a timeline – discuss activity.
2   Be explicit about what skills they should use – talking, looking for evidence, checking ideas, changing things, sequencing, listening to others, sequence the toys.
3   Community of enquiry to discuss the justify their ideas.

Success Criteria
1   To be able to say why they put a toy in a particular place.
2   To sequence the toys on the timeline.

Differentiation
This task is about developing skills and the task is not differentiated except by outcome.

Assessment
Assess children's involvement in the community of enquiry.

2 Thinking skills action plan for 2001/02

Term	Development Focus	Staff Training and Resources	Who	Monitoring Activities	Who	Success Criteria
Au	To improve staff knowledge and understanding of thinking skill strategies	CB to attend Module 1 of Thinking for Learning course (LEA)	CB	Module activities monitored by course tutor	Course Tutor	Confident about the theoretical background of Thinking Skills
	To develop confidence in using strategies in the classroom	WB to attend Philosophy for Children – Level 1 (LEA)	WB	Co-ordinator to observe 1 lesson	LJ	Increase confidence in using strategies across the curriculum
		AH to introduce Top Ten Thinking Tactics to class 3	AH	Observation of Philosophy lesson by co-ordinator	LJ	Begin to introduce Philosophy into the classroom (through stories)
		All teachers to attend training for Thinking Skills Teaching Certificate (Level 1) 2.5 days	All Staff	Pro formas of classroom activities completed after each session – 1 lesson to be observed by a colleague	All Staff	Teachers to be awarded Thinking Skills Teaching Certificate (Level 1)
Sp	To plan use of Thinking Skills strategies into the curriculum	Staff meeting time to begin to plan Thinking Skills into curriculum long-term plan – planning cycle A	All Staff	HT to monitor development of plan	HT	Thinking Skills activities built into long-term curriculum plan (cycle A)
	To increase knowledge of Top Ten Thinking Tactics through Best Practice Research Project	Supply time to organise research programme and complete background reading – support from Newcastle University and LEA.	AH	Individual co-ordinators to monitor development of Thinking Skills in their subject areas	Subject Co-ord	To complete planning of research project and begin to collect data
				Monitored by University of Newcastle research supervisor	New Uni – Viv Baunfield	
Su	To evaluate Thinking Skills activities and collect work to develop portfolio	Staff meetings – share planning of strategies – evaluate sample of lessons – collection of examples of work for portfolios	All Staff	HT and Co-ordinator to collect samples of lesson pro formas. Co-ordinator to collect examples of work and produce portfolio	HT Co-ord	Knowledge of successful strategies for our children
	To share experiences of personal development in Thinking Skills	Staff time to look at development over year and plan ways forward	All Staff	HT and Co-ordinator to arrange and attend moderation and planning meetings with Middle/High Schools	HT Co-ord	Identification of teachers strengths and weaknesses
	Liaison with Middle School/High School – cross phase development	Meetings with Middle/High Schools to plan progression of Thinking Skills strategies across the phases	HT & Co-ord			Thinking Skills portfolio started
						Progression of Thinking Skills activities planned across phases

Byrness First School

1 Geography scheme of work: The Seaside

Learning Objectives Children should learn …	Activities	VAK/ Vocabulary	Learning Outcomes	Resources
Programme of Study	**What are the features of where we live?**			
Identify and describe what places are like.	Go for walk in the school grounds and look at what type of countryside we live in. Mention hills and forests and farms. What type of water we can find in the landscape. Record what we find in our topic books.	Looking around, talking and listening, walking.	Children will recognise and learn the correct terms for the landscape around them.	Countryside around and photocopiable resources.
	What are the features of a city and the seaside and what is the same and what is different?			
Recognise how places compare with other places.	Using the story 'the three bears go to the seaside' and pictures and photographs of the seaside and city talk about what the different landscapes look like. What type of jobs people will do in each area and how the areas are different from each other.	Noticing the differences and applying what they see into questions.	Learn about how different areas look different and have features that are particular to that area.	Story books, pictures and photographs.
	What different sources of water are there in the countryside? Where does a river start and where does it go to?			
Recognise changes in the environment.	Using big book on rivers and supporting materials find out about springs and where reivers start. Follow the river down to the sea.	Linking pictures with information and forming and answering questions	Learn about the journey of a river and how it changes along that journey.	River big book, photocopiable resources and colouring materials.

Learning Objectives Children should learn ...	Activities	VAK/ Vocabulary	Learning Outcomes	Resources
Programme of Study	**What are the special features of the seaside?**			
Identify and describe where places are.	Make a big painting of the seaside with cliffs, sea, sand and a lighthouse. Decorate with under water sea creatures, boats, seabirds and people on the sand. Use the story of the Lighthouse Keeper's lunch as a stimulus.	Painting, cutting and sticking, organising and planning.	Learn and identify the features of the seaside and coastline. Learn the vocabulary and how to spell it.	Stories, pictures, books, Lighthouse Keeper's lunch story.
	What type of jobs do people do at the seaside?			
Recognise changes in human features.	Using photographs and other resources such as our stories and photocopiable resources, talk about and record some of the jobs that people do. Fishermen, coast guards, caravan parks, cafés, shops, hotels, coast protection, harbour master. Talk about which job they would like to do themselves.	Sorting and organising information and making deductions from what they have learned.	Identify the jobs that people do that they will be unable to do elsewhere.	Hopefully will have been on trip so should have hands-on evidence. Use books and photographs as back-up resources.
	What would we need to pack to go on holiday at the seaside?			
Make observations about other features in the environment, e.g. seasonal changes in the weather.	Use a suitcase and various props to put together a suitcase full of useful things to take to the seaside. Talk about what use each thing would be and what activity we would do to need the things we have packed. How are these things different to the things we would normally use? Make a list to make sure we have packed everything when it is time to go home.	Sorting and organising information and making deductions, reasoning why they would need the things they have.	Learn about suitable dressing to do seaside activities, learn about the equipment they would need to have fun.	Suitcase, clothes, sunglasses, sun cream, bucket and spade, inflatable things, swimsuit, towels, etc.
	What activities would we do at the seaside for a week?			
Make observations about where things are located and about other features in the environment.	Using photographs, stories and personal experiences, map out a week's holiday with a visit to the following: a trip in a boat, playing on the sand, visit to the harbour, a walk along the cliffs, a trip to a fun ark or fairground or castle. Reinforce the days of the week and each child to do their own week's holiday.	Planning and sorting a week's holiday using the information they have learned throughout the topic.	Learn about the different activities that the seaside environment offers and how it helps the people who live there.	Timetable, postcards, list of activities and accompanying activities.

193

2 Geography scheme of work: Kenya

Learning Objectives Children should learn ...	Activities	VAK and Vocabulary	Learning Outcomes Children ...
Where are Africa, Kenya and Naro Moru?			
• To investigate places • To respond to geographical questions • To use and interpret globes, atlases and maps • To us secondary sources • To use ICT to access information • To identify physical and human features	• Using globes, world maps, atlases and CD-ROMs, ask the children to locate the position of the UK, Europe, Africa, Kenya and Naro Moru. • Using atlases, maps and aerial photographs of Africa and Kenya ask the children to find out which countries and seas border it and to investigate the weather and climate. • Ask the children to use these resources to add the main physical and human features to a blank map of Kenya. • Produce a whole-class display of a map of Kenya using information collected.	Country, city, hills, rivers, weather, climate, key, symbol, human, physical, landscape V – map of world, Africa, Kenya – labels Posters/photos showing climate A – African music K – handle keywords	• Locate UK and Africa and Kenya • Draw maps to show locational knowledge and awareness of main human and physical features • How is Naro Muru connected to other places? What do we think it will be like?
How is Naro Muru connected to other places? What do we think it will be like?			
• How places relate to each other • To make maps • To use and interpret atlases and maps • To use secondary sources	• Ask the children how they would get to Kenya. Ask them to use atlases, maps and secondary sources to plan a route to Kenya, including information on possible airline routes, distance travelled and countries crosses. They should also note airports they would use. • Discuss with the children what they think Kenya and the village of Naro Moru are like and ask them to list questions relating to what they need to find out to confirm their thoughts.	Village, road route, distance, airport V – look at maps, atlases and plans A – say the route they would take K – Act out plan journey, imaging the sights out of the window	• Prepare a simple map and commentary to show a route to Kenya • Describe what they think Naro Moru village is like
What is the landscape of Naro Moru like?			
• To identify main physical and human features • To make maps	• Discuss with the children, using photographs, what the landscape is like. • Ask them to annotate a base map of Naro Moru, using the picture map and map. Ask them to note the shape of the settlement and the main physical and human features. • Label matching activity.	Settlement, remote, linear, nucleated V – use photographs and keywords A – African music K – Brain gym break – Naro Moru is found in Kenya, Kenya is found in Africa, Africa is next to Europe, UK is found in Europe, and we're from Byrness School (tune – Thigh bones connected to the leg bone ...)	• Complete a map to show the main features of the settlement • Recognise main human and physical features
What are the homes of the children of Naro Moru like?			
• To use secondary sources • About similarities and differences between places	• Group the children and ask them to identify similarities and differences between homes in Naro Moru and those in their locality, using photographs.	Home, houses V – photographs A – last week's tune as brain gym K – pretend to go into the house, go around describing what you see	• Are aware of, and able to discuss, the main similarities and differences in homes

194

Learning Objectives Children should learn ...	Activities	VAK and Vocabulary	Learning Outcomes Children ...
What is the school in Naro Moru like?			
• To use secondary sources • About similarities and differences between places	• Group the children and ask them to discuss and compare photographs of their school with photographs of the school in Naro Moru.	V – photographs A – child's Africa song K – role play being at the school in Naro Moru	• Are aware of, and able to discuss, the main similarities and differences in homes
What is the main type of work in Naro Moru like?			
• To use secondary sources • About similarities and differences between places • To identify land use • To begin to understand the relationship between location and economic activity	• Using photographs, ask the children to describe the work being done. Encourage them to focus on methods of farming, types of crops produced and the work role of women. • Ask them to compare the work people do in Naro Moru with what people do in their locality.	Farming, agriculture, crops, industry, occupation V – keywords A – African music K – role play a work activity done in Naro Moru locality	• Are aware of economic activities • Use aerial photographs to identify and record different forms of land use in and around the village
How do people sell and trade goods in Naro Moru?			
• To use secondary sources • About similarities and differences between places • How places relate to each other	• Ask the children to identify and record the main similarities and differences between a Kenyan local market and a market in their locality, using photographs. • Ask them to think about what they would eat in Naro Moru.	Market, economic activity, trade cash-crop V – keywords A – location song K – sort keywords	• Use secondary sources to identify and record similarities and differences in ways of selling and trading goods • Understand how different places are connected to each other
What are the main similarities and differences between our locality, Nairobi and Naro Moru?			
• About similarities and differences between places • To use ICT to access information	• Use the Internet to gain up-to-date information about, and images of, Kenya. • Ask them to identify and explain the main similarities and differences between their own locality and Naro Moru. • Ask them to reflect on how their ideas about Africa and Kenya have changed and developed. Ask them to list further questions, which, if investigated, would give a more representative view of life in Kenya. • Ask them to produce information posters.	V – pictures and diagrams on the Internet. Information posters A – African music + read information posters K – role play – 'interview' Naro Moru 'inhabitants' to review module	• Review and reflect on what they have found out and how it has affected their initial thinking • Understand ways in which Naro Moru is similar to, and different from, their own locality

All	Should	Could
• About similarities and differences between placesDescribe the main features of the locality • About similarities and differences between placesBegin to recognise difference between localities • About similarities and differences between placesMake simple observations about the locality • About similarities and differences between placesBegin to ask and respond to questions about places, based on their own observation and information provided by the teacher • About similarities and differences between placesUse simple maps and secondary sources	• About similarities and differences between placesDescribe a range of physical and human features of places using appropriate geographical terms • About similarities and differences between placesMake geographical comparisons between localities studies • About similarities and differences between placesOffer appropriate observations about locations of physical and human features • About similarities and differences between placesAsk and respond to geographical questions • About similarities and differences between placesUse of maps and secondary sources	• About similarities and differences between placesMake geographical comparisons and offer reasons for their findings • About similarities and differences between placesBegin to explain 'why things are like that', referring to physical and human features of the landscape • About similarities and differences between placesSuggest appropriate geographical questions for investigation • About similarities and differences between placesUse a range of skills when undertaking an investigation • About similarities and differences between placesInvestigate other places in Kenya and compare these places with Naro Moru and their own locality

Thinking for Learning

3 Lesson plan: geography

Byrness First School – Accelerated Learning Planner

Subject: Teracy/Geography (ICT) **Year** Y2–4

Theme/Topic: Finding and presenting information/Employment in Naro Moru **Time:** 1.25 hrs 9–10.15

- To begin to understand the relationship between location and activity (land use).
- Use aerial photos (Y2), illustrations (Y2) and a range of texts to identify (using scanning and skimming techniques) different forms of employments ir Naor Moru.

Aural questions and use of key vocabulary

Vocab (written), pictures, video + brainstorm

Low Stress – High Challenge

KEY WORDS

Agriculture/crops
Employment
Industry
Occupation
Location
Human features

Link to work on physical features on Kenya and around Naro Moru.

Human features – investigate the employment in the area.

SHARE LEARNING OUTCOMES

INTRODUCE NEW INFORMATION

CONNECT THE LEARNING

The Big Picture

ACTIVITY

REVIEW OF PREVIEW

DEMONSTRATE

De-brief – Has criteria been met?

Next step – Layout and graphics to make a guide using the computer.

Begin – To write a report on findings for a booklet on employment in and around Naro Moru.

- Brainstorm – what work do we think is done in Naro Moru?
- Y2 (+J) = Use photos, pictures, simple given tests video images, etc. to investigate one aspect.
- Y3+4 = Scan texts for key words relating to employment. Choose one aspect, write notes and present information.

Resources

Aerial and other photos, Kenya books, texts for highlighting, highlighter pens, CD Rom(?)

KINSALE AVENUE FIRST SCHOOL

Interim Evaluation Report

<table>
<tr><td colspan="2" align="center">Thinking Schools: Thinking Children
Interim Evaluation Report</td></tr>
<tr><td colspan="2">Areas of focus, e.g. What are your research questions?</td></tr>
<tr><td colspan="2">

1 Is it possible to improve the quality of children's work by increasing the type and amount of feedback they receive?

2 Do all of the children learn effectively if the teacher takes into account different learning styles (visual, auditory and kinesthetic)?

</td></tr>
<tr><td colspan="2">What action have you taken? What evidence did you collect?</td></tr>
<tr><td valign="top">

Feedback

1 Audit – to assess initial position

2 Focus groups/each teacher focused on a lower ability group

3 Use of worksheets for the self-evaluation (happy faces)

4 Child to child feedback, during Circle Time, achievement tree, etc.

5 Teacher feedback – when and how

</td><td valign="top">

Learning styles

1 Audit – to assess initial position

2 Literacy – Pip, Jolly phonics and different types of games

   Numeracy – fans and cards

3 Other subjects, music

</td></tr>
<tr><td colspan="2">What have you learned from this? What has been the impact on the children's learning?</td></tr>
<tr><td valign="top">

Feedback

1 Children had a better idea of what they were expected to achieve

2 Raised self-esteem > raises achievement

3 Raised teachers' awareness of successful learning

</td><td valign="top">

Learning styles

1 Standards in phonics have been greatly improved

2 More access to curriculum for more children

3 Raised teachers' awareness of successful learning

</td></tr>
<tr><td colspan="2">What do you plan to do next?</td></tr>
<tr><td colspan="2">

1 Philosophy through story with Karin Murris

2 Continue work on feedback

3 Continue to develop our teaching styles and review teaching and learning policy

</td></tr>
</table>

Appendix E

HEMPNALL SCHOOL

1 Interim Evaluation Report

<table>
<tr><td colspan="1" align="center">Thinking Schools: Thinking Children
Interim Evaluation Report</td></tr>
<tr><td>Area of focus, e.g. What are your research questions?

If good thinking is shown through debate and discussion does this consequently promote good learning?</td></tr>
<tr><td>What action have you taken? What evidence did you collect?

Logs from the lessons, asking the children about their impression of the lesson. Do the children enjoy these lessons and why. Getting them to identify any differences between story and philosophy.</td></tr>
<tr><td>What have you learned from this?

Thinking time pays off.

In shorter sessions, giving the children a 'thinking task' before reading the story helps focus them.

Use of qualifying language needs to be taught and nutured.</td></tr>
<tr><td>What has been the impact on children's learning?

Children quickly 'cueing' in on discussion skills and listening already improved in these sessions.</td></tr>
<tr><td>What do you plan to do next?

Analyse the questions generated in terms of 'improvement' or development.

Track engagement of quieter members of the group, see if change links to any other self-esteem raising or improvement in other areas.</td></tr>
</table>

2 Interim Evaluation Report

Thinking Schools: Thinking Children
Interim Evaluation Report

Area of focus, e.g. What are your research questions?

If good thinking is shown through debate and discussion does this consequently promote good learning?

What action have you taken? What evidence did you collect?

To ensure drama and Circle Time are timetabled and done
Listened to children's comments
Reflected on their quotes during such sessions
Raised the profile of these areas through displays
I'm asking more questions across the boards (plenary/drama/etc.)

What have you learned from this?

How important it is to give children opportunities to share their ideas by valuing discussion and debate. LISTENING
How this kind of learning approach enabled full participation with children on an equal footing (self-esteem issue)
How unique the children's own ideas are and how I've been able to assess their thinking more

What has been the impact on children's learning?

Children thinking more about consequences, e.g. Does Mother Bear always have to make the porridge?
Extremely positive attitude from children towards such sessions
Children's confidence has grown immensely and self-esteem raised
Children co-operating → school ethos in practice. Across curriculum

What do you plan to do next?

Interview children (self-evaluation)
To collect more evidence through discussions and photographs (possible videos?)
To research/reflect on drama as a learning medium
To link the practical skills used in sessions as evidence of further attainment
Comments analysis 'Are they developing?'

199

ST BENET BISCOP SCHOOL

1 Interim Evaluation Report

Many of the staff at St Benet Biscop School have been developing Thinking for Learning in their departments and classrooms. Below is a selection of some of their ideas from across the curriculum.

English

✴ A Thinking Skills Activity pack is being compiled, containing laminates and assorted tasks. These include the opportunity to solve mysterious crimes; attempt lateral and creative thinking tasks; try out conjuring tricks and crack codes. However, explanations must be given to show their thinking. The tasks encourage deduction, inference, hypothesising, analysis and lateral or creative thinking. These activities can generate high-level vocabulary; encourage children to work collaboratively; exercise narrative and presentational skills and challenge them. These activities have been used with a KS4 group with considerable success and can be used as starter or mid-lesson 'brain boosters'.

✴ In KS3, the department is developing an 'Attack Pack' with the Learning Resource Centre. It will provide a detective trail to help pupils investigate what the centre has to offer.

Science

☺ Many of the staff have been involved in using selected CASE lessons as part of a scheme of work, e.g. 'scaling' in the lessons on the microscope in Year 9, and in 'resistance in electricity and magnetism'. They have also been used to introduce the concept of variables, relationships and fair test in preparation for SC1 investigations.

☺ Living graphs have been introduced into some biology modules.

☺ Mysteries have been used in Year 9 as part of a research project and similar activities have been used to enhance practical work in chemistry and biology.

☺ Odd One Out has been used in chemistry, biology and physics and has been particularly useful for end of module revision.

☺ A 'memory map' has been used to introduce the blast furnace in Years 9 and 10.

Maths

- Year 9 pupils use Thinking Skills activities to classify quadrilaterals through sorting and categorising, applying the appropriate vocabulary from the National Strategy.

- The game 'TABOO' has been used to help KS3 students revise for their SATs and understand number patterns.

- Odd One Out has been incorporated into lessons to help pupils understand units of measurement.

- Year 10 pupils have successfully used Thinking Skills strategies in groups to categorise graphs – quadratic, linear, straight-line and cubic. Building on this, they also worked to sort 'expressions' – such as cubic, quadratic – and 'fractions'. The key focus was to encourage pupils to explain why they had categorised certain groups.

PE

- Thinking Skills have been built into lessons for GCSE and A level. Memory maps, for example, have helped pupils understand the respiratory system at GCSE, and classification tasks have been used successfully at AS level.

HUMANITIES

- Both Year 9 and Year 10 were introduced to concept maps in September 1998 as an introduction to the history and geography course. Pupils helped to generate five basic concepts that they already had about the subject. These concepts were then 'mapped' to begin to explore their understanding of the subject.

- The QCA Kobe Earthquake mystery in geography has been used with Year 9.

- Year 10 have used the Luddite mystery about Joseph Cawthorne in history. The basic question of why Joseph joined the Luddites was explored and linked to a writing frame.

- Odd One Out has been used for various lessons in Years 10, 11 and 12.

- A whole unit on 'Development' was planned for Year 9 geography, using a Thinking Skills approach. Pupil enjoyment and clear understanding were evident.

  The 12 lessons cover:

  - *Defining Development* – using photographs and other images to generate ideas, descriptions and perceptions of development (classification).

  - *Banana Profits* – illustrating economic interdependence and the distribution of profits from the banana industry. Developing feelings of empathy and 'fairness' (causation and interdependence).

  - *Trade Game (Oxfam)* – developing the idea of economic patterns and neo-colonisation. A big emphasis on debriefing and evaluation.

✧ *Debt* – personal analogies (credit cards), international debt (Comic Relief video) and exploration of options.

✧ *Aid* – conclusions leading to written outcomes.

HISTORY

✱ Thinking Skills have been incorporated into a KS3 scheme of work. A variety of strategies are used to engage students in learning, such as the simple stories about Robert Blincoe, which leads to debate; the trial of General Haig, which promotes discussion and argument; and the use of living graphs to help students understand why things happen.

✱ Odd One Out and a Mystery have been used in KS4 and AS.

PSE

✱ Several strategies are being trialled in Year 9, many of them encouraging pupils to make decisions in given situations. Paired work and group tasks enable students to learn to listen to the opinions of others and explain their own viewpoints.

References

1   Adey, P. and Shayer, M. (1994) *Really Raising Standards*, London: Routledge

2   Abbott, J. and Ryan, T. (2000) *The Unfinished Revolution*, Stafford: Network Educational Press

3   QCA (2000) *Religious Education: Non-statutory Guidance*, London

4   Wise, D. and Lovatt, M. (2001) *Creating an Accelerated Learning School*, Stafford: Network Education Press

5   Atkinson, R.L., Atkinson, R.C., Smith, E.E. and Hilgard, E.R. (1987) *Psychology*, San Diego: Harcourt Brace Jovanovich

6   Lipman, M. (1991) *Thinking in Education*, New York: Cambridge University Press

7   Smith, A. (1999) *Accelerated Learning in Practice*, Stafford: Network Educational Press

8   McGuiness, C. (1999) *From Thinking Skills to Thinking Classrooms*, London: DfEE

9   Baumfield, V. (2001) 'Ill thought out thinking skills?', *Teaching Thinking*, winter, 6: 8–9

10 Sharron, H. and Coulter, M. (1987) *Changing Children's Minds*, Birmingham: Imaginative Minds Press

11 Blagg, N. et al. (1985) *Somerset Thinking Skills Course Handbook*, Bristol: Nigel Blagg Associates

12 Adey, P., Shayer, M. and Yates, C. (1993) *Better Learning*, London: Kings College

13 Joyce and Showers (1988) *Student Achievement Through Staff Development*, New York: Longman

14 Leat, D. (1998) *Thinking Through Geography*, Cambridge: Chris Kingston Publications

15 Northumberland County Council (2000) *Thinking for Learning: The Big Picture in Northumberland*, Morpeth, UK: Northumberland County Council

16 Northumberland LEA (1997) *Thinking Skills in the Humanities. A Report on the First Year 1995–96*

17 McGuinness, C., Curry, C., Greer, B., Daly, P. and Salters, M. (1997) *Final Report on the ACTS Project: Phase 2*, Belfast: Northern Ireland Council for Curriculum, Examinations and Assessment

18 Swartz, R. and Parks, S. (1994) *Infusing the Teaching of Critical and Creative Thinking into Content Instruction*, Pacific Grove, CA: Critical Thinking Books and Software

19 SAPERE: The Society for the Advancement of Philosophical Enquiry and Reflection in Education (Sara Liptai, 7 Cloister Way, Leamington Spa, CV32 6QE)

20 Lake, M. and Needham, M. *Top Ten Thinking Tactics*, Birmingham: Questions Publishing

21 Blunkett, B. (2000) 'Raising Aspirations in the 21st Century', speech at the North of England Education Conference, 6 January

22 Barber, M. (1999) At the launch of the McGuinness Report 'From Thinking Skills to Thinking Classrooms', DfEE, May

23 Hughes, M. (1999) *Closing the Learning Gap*, Stafford: Network Educational Press

24 Smith, A. (1996) *Accelerated Learning in the Classroom*, Stafford: Network Educational Press

25 Gardner, H. (1993) *Frames of Mind*, London: Fontana

26 Carroll, L. (1998) 'Jabberwocky', *The Nation's Favourite Poems*, London: BBC Books

27 The Campaign for Learning (2000) *Learning to Learn*, London: The Campaign for Learning

28 Bloom, B. (1956) *The Taxonomy of Educational Objectives*, London: Longman

29 Goleman, D. (1996) *Emotional Intelligence*, London: Bloomsbury

30 Park, J. (2001) 'Thinking with our emotions', *Teaching Thinking*, winter, 6: 34–47

31 Dewey, J. (1997) *How we Think*, Prometheus

32 Brown, A. (1999) *How People Learn*, USA: National Academic Press

33 Swartz, R. (2001) At the 'Breakthroughs 2001: International Conference on Thinking', Auckland, NZ, January

34 Kite, A. (2000) *A Guide to Better Thinking*, Windsor: NFER Nelson

35 Smith, A. and Call, N. (1999) *The ALPS Approach*, Stafford: Network Educational Press

36 Black, P. and Wiliams, D. (1998) *Inside the Black Box*, London: King's College

37 Gipps, C. and Stobart, G. (1993) *Assessment: a Teacher's Guide to the Issues*, London: Hodder and Stoughton

38 Sutton, R. (1995) *Assessment for Learning*, Salford: RS Publications

39 Roberts, N. (2000) *The Integrated Literacy Hour*, Wisbech: Nicholas Roberts Publications

40 Sukhanandan and Lee (1998) *NFER Report: Streaming, Setting and Grouping by Ability. A Review of the Literature*, London: NFER

41 Brown, A. and Campion, J. (1990) 'Communities of Learning and Thinking', *Human Development*, 21 (USA)

42 Fisher, R. (1995) *Teaching Children to Think*, Cheltenham: Stanley Thornes

43 Murris, K. and Haynes, J. (2001) *Storywise*, Newport: Dialogue Works

44 White, E. B. (1963) *Charlotte's Web*, London: Puffin

45 Fullan, M. (1993) *Change Forces*, London: Falmer Press

46 Nottingham, J. (2001) 'RAIS-ing aspirations by teaching thinking?', *Teaching Thinking*, autumn, 5: 32–6

47 Hargreaves, David (2000) *The Guardian*, November

48 Naylor, S. and Keogh, B. (2000) *Concept Cartoons*, Cheshire: Millgate House Publishers

49 Mehl, M. (1985) 'Cognitive difficulties of physics students', PhD Dissertation, University Cape Town

50 Feuerstein and Rand (1977) *Redevelopment of Cognitive Functions in Early Adolescents*, Hadassah Wizo Canada Research Institute

51 Evans, G. (1991) 'The Direct Teaching Of Thinking Skills', *Learning & Teaching Cognitive Skills*, Australian Council for Educational Research.

52 Perkins, D. (1992) *Smart Schools*, New York: Free Press

53 'The National Literacy Strategy: Key Stage 3 Literacy Conference Video 1999', DfEE

Further reading and resources

Abbott, C. and Wilks, S. (1997) *Thinking and Talking Through Literature*, Cheltenham: Hawker Brownlow Education

Adey, P., Shayer, M. and Yates, C. (1995) *A Teacher's Guide to Thinking Science: The Curriculum Materials of the Cognitive Acceleration through Science Education Project*, Nelson

Armstrong, T. (1993) *Seven Kinds of Smart: Identifying and Developing Your Many Intelligences*, New York: Plume

Askew, M., Brown, M., Rhodes, V., Johnson, D. and Wiliam, D. (1997) *Effective Teachers of Numeracy*, London: Kings College, London

Barber, M. (1997) *The Learning Game: Arguments for an Education Revolution*, London: Victor Gollancz

Baumfield, V. M., Leat, D. and Mroz, M. (2000) *Thinking Through Stories*, Newcastle: University of Newcastle

Blagg, N. (1991) *Can We Teach Intelligence?* London: Lawrence Erlbaum

Bowkett, S. (2001) *alps StoryMaker*, Stafford: Network Educational Press

Brearley, M. (2001) *Emotional Intelligence in the Classroom*, Crown House Publishing

Browne, A. (1999) *Voices in the Park*, Corgi

Butler, K. (1984) *Learning and Teaching Style in Theory and Practice*, Columbia: The Learners Dimension

Caine, R. N. and Caine, G. (1991) *Making Connections: Teaching and the Human Brain*, Virginia: ASCD Publications

Cam, P. (1995) *Thinking Together : Philosophical Inquiry for the Classroom*, Sydney: Australian Primary English Teaching Association and Hale & Iremonger

Campbell, K. (1996) *Teaching and Learning through Multiple Intelligences*, Massachusetts: Allyn and Bacon

Carbo, M., Dunn, R. and Dunn, K. (1988) *Teaching Pupils to Read through Their Individual Learning Styles*, New Jersey: Prentice Hall

Caviglioli, O. and Harris, I. (2000) *Mapwise*, Stafford: Network Educational Press

Chapman, C. (1993) *If the Shoe Fits: How to Develop Multiple Intelligences in the Classroom*, Skylight

Claxton, G. (1997) *Hare Brain Tortoise Mind: Why Intelligence Increases When You Think Less*, London: Fourth Estate

Coles, R. (1997) *The Moral Intelligence of Children*, New York: Random House

Cooper, P. and McIntyre, D. (1996) *Effective Teaching and Learning: Teachers' and Students' Perspectives*, Buckingham: Open University Press

Costa, A. (ed) (1991) *Developing Minds: A Resource Book for Teaching Thinking*, Virginia: ASCD Publications

Costa, A. and Kallick, B. (2000) *Habits of Mind*: Virginia: ASCD Publications

Craft, A. (2000) *Creativity Across the Primary Curriculum*, London: Routledge

De Bono, E. (1976) *Teaching Thinking*, Harmondsworth: Penguin

De Haan, C., MacColl, S. and McCutcheon, L. (1995) *Philosophy with Kids, Books 1 to 4*, Melbourne: Longman

Dillon, J. T. (1994) *Using Discussion in Classrooms*, Buckingham: Open University Press

Dryden, G. and Voss, J. (1994) *The Learning Revolution*, Stafford: Network Educational Press

Egan, K. (1992) *Imagination in Teaching and Learning: Ages 8 to 15*, London: Routledge

Feuerstein, R., Rand, Y., Hoffman, M. and Miller, R. (1980) *Instrumental Enrichment*, Baltimore: University Park Press

Fisher, R. (1991) *Teaching Children to Think*, London: Stanley Thornes

Fisher, R. (1995) *Teaching Children to Learn*, London: Stanley Thornes

Fisher, R. (1996) *Stories for Thinking*, Nash Pollock

Fisher, R. (1997) *Poems for Thinking*, Nash Pollock

Fisher, R. (1997) *Games for Thinking*, Nash Pollock

Fisher, R. (1998) *Teaching Thinking: Philosophical Enquiry in the Classroom*, London: Cassell

Fisher, R. (1999) *First Stories for Thinking*, Nash Pollock

Fisher, R. (2000) *First Poems for Thinking*, Nash Pollock

Fisher, R. (2001) *Values for Thinking*, Nash Pollock

Fullan, M. (1999) *Change Forces, The Sequel*, London: Falmer Press

Gardner, H. (1993) *Multiple Intelligences: The Theory in Practice*, New York: Basic Books

Gardner, H. (1993) *The Unschooled Mind*, London: Fontana

Gardner, H. (1999) *The Disciplined Mind: What all Students Should Know and Understand*, New York: Simon and Shuster

Goleman, D. (1998) *Working with Emotional Intelligence*, London: Bloomsbury

Higgins, S. and Downey, G. (2001) *Thinking Through Mental Calculation*, Newcastle: University of Newcastle

Howard, P. J. (1994) *The Owner's Manual for the Brain – Everyday Applications for Mind-Brain Research*, Texas: Bard Press

Jensen, E. (1995) *Super Teaching*, San Diego: The Brain Store

Jensen, E. (1995) *Brain-Based Learning and Teaching*, California: Turning Point

Jensen, E. (1998) *Teaching with the Brain in Mind*, Virginia: ASCD Publications

Lazear, D. (1993) *Seven Ways of Teaching: The Artistry of Teaching with Multiple Intelligences*, Zephyr Press

LeDoux, J. (1998) *The Emotional Brain*, London: Wiedenfield and Nicholson

Lipman, M. and Sharp, A. (1978) *Growing up with Philosophy*, Philadelphia: Temple University Press

Lipman, M. and Sharp, A. (1980) *Philosophy in the Classroom*, Philadelphia: Temple University Press

Lipman, M. (1988) *Philosophy Goes to School*, Philadelphia : Temple University Press

Lipman, M. (ed) (1993) *Thinking Children and Education,* Dubuque: Kendall/Hunt

Matthews, G. B. (1980) *Philosophy and the Young Child,* Cambridge: Harvard University Press

Matthews, G. B. (1984) *Dialogues with Children*, Cambridge: Harvard University Press

Matthews, G. B. (1994) *The Philosophy of Childhood*, Cambridge: Harvard University Press

Nisbet, J and Shucksmith, J. (1986) *Learning Strategies,* London: Routledge/Kegan Paul

O'Connor, J. and Seymour, J. (1995) *Introducing Neuro-Linguistic Programming*, London: Thorsons

Perkins, D. (1995) *Outsmarting IQ: The Emerging Science of Learnable Intelligence*, New York: The Free Press

Pritchard, M. (1996) *Reasonable Children: Moral Education and Moral Learning*, Lawrence: University Press of Kansas

Quinn, V. (1997) *Critical Thinking in Young Minds*, London: David Fulton

Reed, R. F. (1983) *Talking with Children*, Denver: Arden Press

Rose, C. and Nicholl, M. J. (1997) *Accelerated Learning for the 21st Century*, New York: Delacorte Press

Ryle, G. (1982) *On Thinking*, Oxford: Blackwell

Smith, A. and Call, N. (2001) *The alps Approach Resource Book*, Stafford: Network Educational Press

Sprod, T. (1993) *Books into Ideas*, Cheltenham: Hawker Brownlow Education

Splitter, L. and Sharp, A. M. (1995) *Teaching for Better Thinking: The Classroom Community of Inquiry*, Hawthorn: Australian Council for Educational Research

Steiner, C. (1997) *Achieving Emotional Literacy*, New York: Avon Books

Sternberg, R. J. (1996) *Successful Intelligence: How Practical and Creative Intelligence Determine Success in Life*, New York: Plume

Sutcliffe, R. and Williams, S. *The Philosophy Club: An Adventure in Thinking*, Newport: Dialogue Works

Sutcliffe, R. and Williams, S. *Newswise: Thinking through the News*, Newport: Dialogue Works

Vygotsky, L. S. (1978) *Mind in Society*, Cambridge: Harvard University Press

Wilks, S. (1995) *Critical & Creative Thinking: Strategies for Classroom Inquiry*, Armadale: Eleanor Curtain

Top thinking websites

www.alite.co.uk	accelerated learning news, case studies and training
www.campaign-for-learning.org	website promoting lifelong learning
www.thethinkingclassroom.co.uk	thinking classrooms in practice
www.education-quest.com	Teaching Thinking journal's site
www.sapere.net	website of the Society for the Advancement of Philosophical Enquiry and Reflection in Education
www.thinkingcap.org.uk	P4C website
www.dialogueworks.co.uk	P4C website
www.nelig.com	national emotional literacy interest group's official site
www.antidote.org.uk	an organisation working to create an emotionally literate society
www.cherylbuggy.co.uk	website of Discovery's project director
www.eiconsortium.org/members/goleman.htm	Daniel Goleman and his work
www.pz.harvard.edu/Default.htm	Harvard's Project Zero homepage, detailing the work of such researchers as Howard Gardner and David Perkins
www.psych.qub.ac.uk/staff/mcguinness.html	Carol McGuinness and her work
www.teachingthinking.net	Robert Fisher's website
www.kcl.ac.uk/depsta/education/teaching/CASE.html	CASE website
www.edwdebono.com	Edward de Bono/CoRT
www.yale.edu/pace/teammembers/personalpages/bob.html	Robert Sternberg and his work
www.mind-map.com	Tony Buzan's website
www.ncl.ac.uk/education/research/li/tsrc/research.html	University of Newcastle's Thinking Skills research centre
www.scre.ac.uk/rie/nl68/nl68kite.html	Anne Kite's report on how to help children become effective thinkers and learners
www.nwrel.org/scpd/sirs/6/cu11.html	the North West Regional Educational Laboratory's (NWREL) report into Thinking skills

http://edservices.aea7.k12.ia.us/framework/thinking

thinking materials from a US Education Agency

http://members.ozemail.com.au/~caveman/Creative/Techniques

practical strategies for use in the classroom

www.cre8ng.com/CC/cc99/index99.html — creative challenges for students

www.nea.org/helpfrom/connecting/tools/thinking.html#intro

the American National Education Association's site on how parents can help children with Thinking Skills

www.schoolexpress.com/fws/sub_cat1ThinkingSkills.asp?cat=ThinkingSkills

free Thinking Skills worksheet

http://eric.indiana.edu — Educational Resources Information Centre (English and Communication) website, containing critical thinking resources

http://falcon.jmu.edu/~ramseyil/critical.htm — list of sites for critical thinking and problem-solving skills (includes general information, lesson plans and bibliography)

www.tuckswoodfirst.norfolk.sch.uk — a thinking school website

www.criticalthinking.com — commercial site for books and software

◆ INDEX

Other publications in The Accelerated Learning Series

General editor: Alistair Smith

Book 1: Accelerated Learning in Practice by Alistair Smith

ISBN: 1 855 39 048 5 Paperback   ISBN: 1 855 39 068x Hardback

- ◆ The author's second book that takes Nobel Prize winning brain research into the classroom.
- ◆ Structured to help readers access and retain the information necessary to begin to accelerate their own learning and that of the students they teach.
- ◆ Contains over 100 learning tools, case studies from 36 schools and an up-to-the-minute section.
- ◆ Includes 9 principles of learning based on brain research and the author's 7-stage Accelerated Learning cycle.

Book 2: the alps approach: accelerated learning in primary schools by Alistair Smith and Nicola Call

ISBN: 1 885 39 056 6 Paperback   ISBN: 1 885 39 066 3 Hardback

- ◆ Shows how research on how we learn, collected by Alistair Smith, can be used to great effect in the primary classroom.
- ◆ Provides practical and accessible examples of strategies used by highly experienced primary teach Nicola Call, at a school where the SATs results shot up as a consequence.
- ◆ Professional, practical and exhilarating resource that gives readers the opportunity to develop the ALPS approach for themselves and for the children in their care.
- ◆ The ALPS approach includes: Exceeding expectations, 'Can-do' learning, Positive performance, Target-setting that works, Using review for recall, Preparing for tests … and much more.

Book 3: Mapwise by Oliver Caviglioli and Ian Harris

ISBN: 1 855 39 059 0 Paperback   ISBN: 1 855 39 060 4 Hardback

- ◆ Infuses thinking skills into subject delivery.
- ◆ Supports each stage of the accelerated learning process.
- ◆ Can be used to measure and develop intelligence.
- ◆ Supports pupils of all learning styles in developing their essential learning skills.
- ◆ Supports teacher explanation and pupil understanding
- ◆ Makes teach planning, teaching and reviewing easier and more effective.

Book 4: the alps resource book by Alistair Smith and Nicola Call

ISBN: 1 885 39 078 7

A follow-up to the best-selling alps approach, it provides photocopiable resource for teachers to use in the classroom.

- Affirmation posters for the classroom
- The 100 best homeworks
- How to make target setting easy, fun and useful
- Writing frames and thinking skills templates
- 101 Brain Break activities that connect to learning
- Lists of the best music for learning

Book 5: Creating an Accelerated Learning School

ISBN: 1 885 39 074 4 Paperback   ISBN: 1 885 39 053 1 Hardback

A follow-up to the best-selling alps approach, it provides photocopiable resource for teachers to use in the classroom.

- The need for accelerated learning
- Establishing accelerated learning within the school
- Supporting and embedding accelerated learning
- OFSTED and beyond

Book 6: alps StoryMaker - with double dare gang book 1 and 2

ISBN: 1 885 39 076 0

- Insights into the nature of creativity and how to be systematic in developing a creative attitude to generate useful ideas across a broad field of contexts
- Ways of raising awareness of and practising an extensive menu of thinking skills
- Techniques for processing information from any subject more effectively
- Activities which boost the 'intelligence behaviours' that characterise effective learners

Book 7: The Brain's Behind It

ISBN: 1 885 39 083 3

Alistair Smith guides the reader through the development cycle of the brain and then describes what helps and hinders learning.

- How do I help my child improve at maths?
- What is the best time for my child to begin formal learning?
- Why will the children in my class not sit still?
- Can you teach intelligence?
- How does sleep improve all-round memory and recall?
- Should we teach boys and girls separetely?
- What is memory? Does it exist somewhere in the brain?
- What does brain science tell us about selection by ability?

Reaching Out To All Learners

ISBN: 1 885 39 143 0

This booklet is intended as an aide-memoire for classroom teachers on some of the basic principles of Accelerated Learning, and useful sources and resources.

◆ 10 great ideas for sustaining the Mind Friendly Learning Framework in your school
◆ Powerful facts about learning
◆ The essential details about memory review, recall and retention
◆ Useful websites

Bright Sparks: Motivational Posters for Pupils by Alistair Smith

ISBN: 1 885 39 088 4

Over 100 photocopiable posters to help motivate pupils and help improve their learning.

◆ The magic spelling strategy
◆ How you learn best
◆ The abc of motivation
◆ Exam technique

Leading Learning: Staff Development Posters for Schools by Alistair Smith

ISBN: 1 885 39 089 2

With over 200 posters which draw from the best in brain research from around the world.

◆ 5 features of learning to learn
◆ Smart marking
◆ Target setting
◆ Effective lesson structures
◆ Thinking skills

Forthcoming titles in The Accelerated Learning Series

Becoming Emotionally Intelligent   Cath Corrie
Accelerated Learning in the Early Years   Nicola Call

Other series from Network Educational Press

THE SCHOOL EFFECTIVENESS SERIES

Book 1:   *Accelerated Learning in the Classroom* by Alistair Smith

Book 2:   *Effective Learning Activities* by Chris Dickinson

Book 3:   *Effective Heads of Department* by Phil Jones & Nick Sparks

Book 4:   *Lessons are for Learning* by Mike Hughes

Book 5:   *Effective Learning in Science* by Paul Denley and Keith Bishop

Book 6:   *Raising Boys' Achievement* by Jon Pickering

Book 7:   *Effective Provision for Able & Talented Children* by Barry Teare

Book 8:   *Effective Careers Education & Guidance* by Andrew Edwards and Anthony Barnes

Book 9:   *Best behaviour and Best behaviour FIRST AID* by Peter Relf, Rod Hirst, Jan Richardson and Georgina Youdell

   Best behaviour FIRST AID
   (pack of 5 booklets)

Book 10:   *The Effective School Governor* by David Marriott
   (including free audio tape)

Book 11:   *Improving Personal Effectiveness for Managers in Schools* by James Johnson

Book 12:   *Making Pupil Data Powerful* by Maggie Pringle and Tony Cobb

Book 13:   *Closing the Learning Gap* by Mike Hughes

Book 14:   *Getting Started* by Henry Leibling

Book 15:   *Leading the Learning School* by Colin Weatherley

Book 16:   *Adventures in Learning* by Mike Tilling

Book 17:   *Strategies for Closing the Learning Gap* by Mike Hughes with Andy Vass

Book 18:   *Classroom Management* by Philip Waterhouse and Chris Dickinson

Book 19:   *Effective Teachers* by Tony Swainston

EDUCATION PERSONNEL MANAGEMENT SERIES

These new Education Personnel Management handbooks will help headteachers, senior managers and governors to manage a broad range of personnel issues.

The Well Teacher – management strategies for beating stress, promoting staff health and reducing absence
by Maureen Cooper

Managing Challenging People – dealing with staff conduct
by Bev Curtis and Maureen Cooper

Managing Poor Performance – handling staff capability issues
by Bev Curtis and Maureen Cooper

Managing Allegations Against Staff – personnel and child protection issues in schools
by Maureen Cooper

Managing Recruitment and Selection – appointing the best staff
by Bev Curtis and Maureen Cooper

Managing Redundancies – dealing with reduction and reorganisation of staff
by Bev Curtis and Maureen Cooper

Paying Staff in Schools – performance management and pay in schools
by Bev Curtis

VISIONS OF EDUCATION SERIES

The Unfinished Revolution by John Abbott and Terry Ryan

The Child is Father of the Man by John Abbott

The Learning Revolution by Jeanette Vos and Gordon Dryden
    The book includes a huge wealth of data and research from around the world.

Wise-Up by Guy Claxton

THE LITERACY COLLECTION

Class Talk by Rosemary Sage

COGS (Communication Opportunity Group Scheme) by Rosemary Sage

Thinking for Learning

THE NUMERACY COLLECTION

Numeracy Activities - plenary, practical & problem solving - Key Stage 2 by
Afzal Ahmed and Honor Williams

Numeracy Activities - plenary, practical & problem solving - Key Stage 3 by
Afzal Ahmed, Honor Williams and George Wickham

OTHER TITLES FROM NEP

Effective Resources for Able and Talented Children by Barry Teare

More Effective Resources for Able and Talented Children by Barry Teare

Imagine That... by Stephen Bowkett

Self-Intelligence by Stephen Bowkett

Thinking Skills and Eye Q by Oliver Caviglioli, Ian Harris and Bill Tindall

Brain Friendly Revision by University of First Age

Teaching Pupils how to Learn - research, practice and INSET resources
by Bill Lucas, Toby Greany, Jill Rodd and Ray Wicks

Tweak to Transform by Mike Hughes with David Potter